How to answer a MORMON

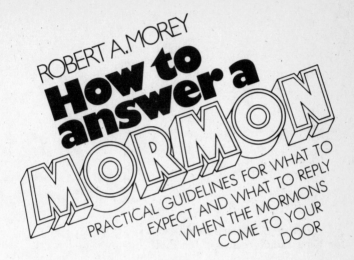

ROBERT A. MOREY

How to answer a MORMON

PRACTICAL GUIDELINES FOR WHAT TO EXPECT AND WHAT TO REPLY WHEN THE MORMONS COME TO YOUR DOOR

BETHANY HOUSE PUBLISHERS
MINNEAPOLIS, MINNESOTA 55438
A Division of Bethany Fellowship, Inc.

All Scripture quotations have been taken from
the King James Version of the Bible.

Copyright © 1983
Robert A. Morey
All Rights Reserved

Published by Bethany House Publishers
A Division of Bethany Fellowship, Inc.
6820 Auto Club Road, Minneapolis, Minnesota 55438

Printed in the United States of America

Library of Congress Cataloging in Publication Data

Morey, Robert A., 1946-
   How to answer a Mormon.

   1. Mormon Church—Doctrinal and controversial works.
I. Title.
BX8645.M59   1983   230'.93   82-24315
ISBN 0-87123-260-X

I wish to give special acknowledgment to Donna Shadel and Dave Helmus for their gracious assistance in the preparation of this manuscript.

ABOUT THE AUTHOR

Dr. Robert Morey has earned degrees in philosophy, theology and apologetics. He is listed in *The International Authors and Writers Who's Who*, and *Contemporary Writers* and is presently Executive Director of the Research and Education Foundation. His books (some have been translated into Spanish, German, French and Chinese) include:

Death and the Afterlife
When Is It Right to Fight?
A Christian Handbook for Defending the Faith
Horoscopes and the Christian
Reincarnation and Christianity
How to Answer a Mormon
How to Answer a Jehovah's Witness
The Saving Work of Christ
Worship Is All of Life
The Bible and Drug Abuse
The Dooyeweerdian Concept of the Word of God
An Examination of Exclusive Psalmody
Is Sunday the Christian Sabbath?
Outlines for Living

TABLE OF CONTENTS

Part 1

THE CHRISTIAN CHURCH
AND THE MORMONS

Beginning with only six members in 1830, Mormonism has increased in membership to almost five million worldwide, and is gaining thousands of converts every year. The annual *Yearbook of American and Canadian Churches* reveals that some of the Mormon churches are experiencing the highest and most consistent growth patterns of any major religious body in the U.S.

While there are two major Mormon denominations (the Utah Latter-Day Saints Church and the Missouri Reorganized Church) and several smaller splinter groups (The Church of Christ of the Temple Lot, etc.), the Utah-based Church of Jesus Christ of Latter-Day Saints is the largest and most aggressive in seeking converts. Unless a person happens to live in the Midwest, the Mormon missionaries who come to his door are usually members of the L.D.S. Church.

The Mormon religion has splintered into various organizations because of major disagreements over doctrine. Two significant areas of disagreement between the Utah L.D.S. Church and the Missouri Reorganized Church center in the issues of polytheism and polygamy. While the L.D.S. Church teaches polytheism and practiced polygamy at one time, the Reorganized Church is monotheistic and presently rejects polygamy.

The L.D.S. Church is the fastest growing Mormon Church. Its tremendous growth is due to its missionary program, which involves the youth of the church in a two-year missionary outreach at their own expense. Every year thousands of young Mormons graduate from high school and spend their next two years as missionaries for their church. With an annual crop of new missionaries, the Mormon leaders can designate a target area and send thousands of missionaries to saturate the area with Mormon literature. It is no surprise that this method is so successful.

Because of the Mormon missionary strategy of saturating an area, many Christians are being confronted by these zealous disciples of Joseph Smith. Yet, most Christians do not know how to handle Mormon missionaries. What should they say when the Mormons come knocking? What subject should they discuss with these clean-cut, neatly dressed young people?

1. *A Christian needs to understand what a "cult" is.*

A "cult" is a religious organization founded by and built upon the teachings of a religious leader whose authority is viewed as being equal to or greater than the Bible and whose teachings are in opposition to the doctrines of biblical and historic Christianity.

The crucial part of the above definition of the word cult is, "whose authority is viewed as being equal to or greater than the Bible." The founder of the cult is viewed as being a "prophet" or "prophetess" of God. Since he or she is the "voice of God," the person's teachings are authoritative. Thus the cult is based solely upon the religious authority of the founder. Everything depends on the validity of that authority.

The issue of religious authority is the most basic problem one encounters when witnessing to a cultist. While the child of God looks to the Scriptures as the ultimate standard by which to decide religious truth, the cultist looks to his leader to decide the truth for him. As long as the Christian and the cultist are looking to different religious authorities, there is no common ground between them where they can begin.

2. *A Christian must understand that Mormonism is a cult.*

In the light of our definition of the word "cult," it is abundantly clear that Mormonism is a "cult" and not a Christian church or denomination, because it is built entirely on Joseph Smith. The authority of the Mormon priesthood and the validity of their doctrines rest totally on Joseph Smith's claim to be an inspired prophet of God. He is their *only* basis of religious authority.

3. *A Christian must realize that the real problem which must be dealt with when witnessing to a Mormon is the question of religious authority.*

Despite the doctrinal differences between the various Mormon groups, they are united on one point: *they believe and teach that Joseph Smith is a prophet of God.* He is the basis of their religious authority.

> By hundreds of thousands in many lands Joseph Smith is today held in remembrance as a prophet of God. . . . The Church of Jesus Christ of Latter-Day Saints has its foundation in the revelations he received, the sacred truths he taught, and the authority of the priesthood restored through him. (*Joseph Smith's Testimony*, p. 30)

The sum and substance of Mormonism can be found in two words: "Joseph Smith." Since the foundation of the church rests entirely on his validity as a true prophet of God, he becomes the "Achilles' heel" of the Mormon religion.

> If his claims to divine appointment be false, forming as they do the foundation of the Church . . . the superstructure cannot be stable. . . . (*Articles of Faith*, L.D.S., pp. 7-8)

When confronting a cultist, the worst thing we can do is to deal with peripheral issues. This is generally a waste of time and utterly fruitless in bringing the cultist to a saving knowledge of Jesus Christ. Thus one should not argue over blood transfusion with Jehovah's Witnesses or polygamy with L.D.S. Mormons. One needs to go right to *the* crucial issue when dealing with a cultist.

When confronted by Mormon missionaries, it is soon obvious that they are well-trained and prepared to discuss their church's doctrines. They will gladly discuss their "restored gospel," the Mormon priesthood, why they build temples, baptism for the dead, eternal marriages, etc. And, sad to say, many Christians will follow the leading of the Mormon missionaries in dealing with these sticky, but nonessential issues.

The only issue which the Mormons are not well-prepared to discuss, with any measure of knowledge, is the issue of Joseph Smith's claim to be a true prophet of God. Although these missionaries have memorized their "missionary handbook" and have practiced their presentation and arguments, they are not ready to deal with this issue because it is not dealt with in their manual.

4. *A Christian should initially deal with only one issue when confronting Mormons. This crucial issue is Joseph Smith's claim to be a true prophet of God.*

A Mormon missionary is trained to give a "testimony" in which he or she states, "I testify by the Spirit of God that I know that Joseph Smith was a prophet of God and that the *Book of Mormon* is the Word of God." They will repeat this statement continually much like a Muslim says, "Allah is God and Mohammed is his prophet." They have memorized this testimony from their manual.

Although they are trained to give their "witness" with great sincerity and conviction, it is a prime example of circular reasoning. After the Mormon says, "I testify that Joseph Smith is a prophet of God," the Christian should ask, "How do you *know* that he was a prophet of God?" The Mormon will reply, "Because God spoke to him." The Christian should then ask, "How do you *know* that God spoke to him?" The Mormon will respond, "Because he was a prophet of God." The Mormon ends up giving a circular argument.

The Christian must call the Mormon's attention to his circular reasoning and then ask him, "How do you *know* that Joseph Smith was a prophet to whom God spoke?" The Mormon will respond, "Because I have a burning witness in my heart. I got on my knees and asked God to show me if Joseph Smith was His prophet and the Book of Mormon was inspired. And now I have a burning *feeling* in my heart that these things are true."

The Christian must point out that all religions and cults claim that their "heart" or "feelings" tell them that they are "right." What if an Adventist, a Jehovah's Witness, a Moonie or a follower of Rev. Ike were present in the same room as the Mormons? Wouldn't they *all* claim a subjective inner witness to the truthfulness of their particular cult? It must be pointed out to the Mormon that his argument from subjective feelings is just as invalid as was his use of circular reasoning.

Mormon missionaries are trained to ask, "What do you *feel* about the *Book of Mormon*? Our family night program?" etc. They will always seek to direct the prospective convert to his or her *feelings*. They do this in order to keep the person from *thinking* about things. Thus the Christian must respond by pointing out that "feelings" should not determine truth. We need to *think rationally* about the issues which the Mormons raise and to seek the *facts* which will determine the outcome.

The 1973 Mormon missionary handbook uses the word "feelings" or "feel" on the average of two or three times a page. The Christian must not be trapped into discussing his feelings instead of Joseph Smith's claim to prophethood.

At this point, the Christian should say, "Listen, we must have an *objective* way to *test* whether Joseph Smith was really a prophet. Since there are dozens of people who claim to be 'a prophet of God,' there must be some way to distinguish between true and false prophets."

In the Mormon book, *Doctrines of Salvation* (p. 188), Joseph Fielding Smith, a past president and prophet of the Mormon Church, states that Joseph Smith's claim to divine prophethood must be tested by *Scripture*. The Christian heartily agrees with the Mormons on this point. The Mormon should be shown this document to encourage him to turn to Scripture as the test. This document is reproduced in Part 2 of this book, on page 28.

5. *The most effective but simple way to test Joseph Smith's claim to be a prophet of God is to examine his prophecies.*

What do we get from prophets? We get prophecies. This means that we should examine the prophecies of Joseph Smith.

Some Mormons have claimed that Joseph Smith never gave any prophecies. Our response is to point out that a prophet who never gives any prophecies is an impossibility. Have they ever heard of a banana salesman who never had any bananas to sell? Or, a car salesman who never had any cars?

Only inexperienced Mormons would ever seek to deceive people into thinking that Joseph Smith never made any prophecies. An educated Mormon will admit that Smith made prophecies.

The Christian must firmly establish that we can objectively test the claim of Joseph Smith by examining his prophecies. Have the Mormon turn to Deut. 18:20-22. Since

Smith himself "translated" the passage in his "inspired" version, it has full authority for Mormons.

> But the prophet, which shall presume to speak a word in my name, which I have not commanded him to speak, or that shall speak in the name of other gods, even that prophet shall die. And if thou say in thine heart, How shall we know the word which the Lord hath not spoken? When the prophet speaketh in the name of the Lord, if the thing follow not, nor come to pass, that is the thing which the Lord hath not spoken, but the prophet hath spoken it presumptuously: thou shalt not be afraid of him.

The logic of this biblical passage is very simple. If someone claims to be a prophet of God but his predictions fail to happen, this person is a false prophet. This line of logic should be repeated to the Mormon until he understands it.

6. *When the prophecies of Joseph Smith are examined, it can be demonstrated that he was a false prophet.*

With surprising ease, a Christian can guide a Mormon up to this point. Now the hard work begins because the Mormon is on very shaky ground. He was never trained to deal with Smith's prophecies. The Mormon leaders discourage members from studying such things. Because the Mormon is unsure of himself, the Christian can lovingly take over and lead him to examine the prophecies of Smith. Do not argue over doctrine or peripheral issues. Keep to the one issue of Smith's prophecies. Keep stressing that the historic documents have the last word and that they have priority over guesses and speculations. The issue is one of *facts*, not theories.

HOW TO USE THE INFORMATION GIVEN IN PART 2

Part 2 of this book contains the documentation for some of the false prophecies of Joseph Smith. Although there are over sixty obviously false prophecies made by Joseph

Smith, the ones which are included in Part 2 are the most useful. There are several things to remember as you use them.

1. The prophecies from *Doctrine and Covenants* come from an "inspired" book of the Mormons. Each "inspired" revelation is dated and numbered. They usually begin by saying, "Thus says the Lord." Thus they are *not* mere opinions or guesses made by Smith but "inspired" prophecies. This must be stressed to the Mormon.

2. Since the Bible came *before* the *Book of Mormon, The Pearl of Great Price* and *Doctrine and Covenants*, it will judge all new revelations. Thus Deut. 18:20-22 applies directly to Smith's prophecies.

3. False prophecies are not "mistakes." We all make mistakes but most of us never claimed to be a "prophet of God" who speaks "inspired revelations." To equate false prophecies with mistakes is like equating apples and shoestrings. There is no logical connection.

4. Let the Mormon read Smith's prophecies in their entirety, if he so pleases. We have photostatically reproduced the entire page so as to avoid the charge, "You are taking these prophecies out of context." The context is reproduced to allow a fair reading of the prophecy.

5. Go through all the material. Don't let the Mormon escape by allowing him to brush aside Smith's prophecies as unimportant. Keep pointing out to him that the only *real* issue between Christianity and Mormonism is whether or not Joseph Smith was a true or false prophet. Be prepared for the Mormon to attempt to change the subject to an issue he is prepared to discuss. Keep to the *one issue* of Joseph Smith's claim to be a prophet.

6. Be prepared to respond to the "pat answers" which Mormon missionaries are told to give when confronted by the false prophecies of Joseph Smith:

MORMON: *"Smith never made any prophecies."*
YOUR RESPONSE: *Doctrine and Covenants* and *The*

Pearl of Great Price record many of Smith's prophecies. Mormon bookstores even sell books on Smith's prophecies.

MORMON: *"Smith was only giving his personal opinion. He wasn't speaking as a prophet."*

YOUR RESPONSE: Each prophecy recorded in *Doctrine and Covenants* is a numbered and dated revelation from God. Smith's predictions begin with "Thus says the Lord" and full inspiration is claimed for each one.

MORMON: *"If Smith was a false prophet, so was Moses. Didn't he predict that he would lead Israel into the Promised Land? Yet he died on the other side of Jordan."*

YOUR RESPONSE: The God who originally *commanded* Moses to lead Israel out of Egypt (Ex. 3:10) later *prophesied* that Moses was to die before entering the land as a punishment for sin (Num. 20:12). Moses' death fulfills this prophecy (Deut. 34:5). Thus to construe Moses' death as a false prophecy is impossible. Nowhere did Moses ever prophesy that he would enter the land.

MORMON: *"If Smith was a false prophet, then so was Christ. Didn't He prophesy that His second coming would take place in that generation and that there were those living who would not die before His return?"*

YOUR RESPONSE: No, Christ never prophesied that His second coming would take place in the generation in which He lived. *First,* His prophecy in Matt. 24:34 referred to the generation of the end times, not of Jesus' time. The main question Jesus was answering in this passage was, "What shall be the sign of thy coming, and of the end of the world?" (v. 3). Jesus then enumerated the events which would precede His second advent. When He noted that "this generation shall not pass, till all these things be fulfilled," He was referring to the generation that will witness these signs of the last days. *Second,* Christ's prophecy in Luke 9:27 was fulfilled by the establishment of the Church. Matthew Henry writes,

"They saw the kingdom of God when the Spirit was poured out, when the gospel was preached to all the world and nations were brought to Christ by it."

7. Once all of Smith's prophecies have been examined, the Mormon needs to hear the biblical gospel. We must remember that the climax of the presentation is the gospel of Christ. Here the Mormon can be led to accept Jesus Christ as his personal Lord and Savior. Conclude your discussion with a plea for him to test his "feelings" by Scripture. Challenge him to look up the documents for himself and not to accept a "pat" answer from his leaders.

8. Encourage the Mormon to contact the ex-Mormon organizations and correspond with them as to why they left the Mormon Church. Since he will have been taught much false doctrine, lend him a Christian book which refutes Mormon doctrine. The names of these organizations and books are listed on the next page.

Conclusion

The ultimate goals of this presentation are the conversion of thousands of Mormons and the preventive inoculation of thousands of Christians and non-Christians as to why they should not become Mormons. The method which is presented in this book does not require a detailed knowledge of Mormon history or doctrine. It does not require a knowledge of Greek or Hebrew. A layperson can easily retain and use the argument that the false prophecies of Joseph Smith totally discredit his claim to be God's inspired prophet. May God bless this presentation and use it to the benefit of many.

WHERE TO TURN FOR FURTHER HELP

I. *Organizations to Contact*

BOISE CHRISTIAN OUTREACH
Box 3356
Boise, Ida. 83703

CHRISTIAN APOLOGETICS PROJECT
Box 105
Absecon, N.J. 08201

MORMON RESEARCH MINISTRY
Box 20705
El Cajon, Calif. 92021

CHRISTIAN RESEARCH INSTITUTE
Box 500
San Juan Capistrano, Calif. 92075

EX-MORMONS FOR JESUS

SAINTS ALIVE
Box 1076
Issaquah, Wash. 98027

WEST COAST
Box 1322
Garden Grove, Calif. 92642

CENTRAL OFFICE
Box 312-13
Wheeling, Ill. 60090

EASTERN OFFICE
Box 946
Safety Harbor, Fla. 33572

GOSPEL TRUTH
Box 2850
Mission Viejo, Calif. 92690

MARQUARDT
445 E. Pioneer Ave.
Sandy, Utah 84070

MISSION TO MORMONS
Box 322
Roy, Utah 84067

MODERN MICROFILM CO.
Box 1884
Salt Lake City, Utah 84110

MacGREGOR MINISTRIES
Box 1215
Delta, B.C.
Canada, V4M 373

PERSONAL FREEDOM OUTREACH
Box 26062
St. Louis, Mo. 63136

UTAH MINISTRIES, INC.
Box 348
Marlow, Okla. 73055

WATCHMAN FELLOWSHIP
Box 7681
Columbus, Ga. 31908

II. *Resource Material in Print.*

The organizations above will usually have their own assortment of tracts and books. The following books can be obtained from a local Christian bookstore.

— Biderwolf, W., *Mormonism Under the Searchlight*, Eerdmans.

— Cowdrey, Davis & Scales, *Who Really Wrote the Book of Mormon?* Vision House, 1977.

— Cowan, M., *Mormon Claims Answered*, 1975.

— Hoekema, A., *The Four Major Cults*, Eerdmans, 1971.

— Fraser, G., *Is Mormonism Christian?*, Moody Press, 1977.

— Martin, W., *The Maze of Mormonism*, Vision House, 1978.

— Martin, W., *Mormonism*, Bethany House, 1976.

— Ropp, H., *The Mormon Papers*, InterVarsity, 1977.

— Tanner, J. & S., *The Changing World of Mormonism*, Moody Press, 1980.

— Scott, L., *The Mormon Mirage*, Zondervan, 1979.

Part 2

THE PROPHECIES OF JOSEPH SMITH

Joseph Smith's claim to be a true prophet of God must be considered seriously by anyone who desires to know and to do God's will in these latter days. His claims are so astounding that there are only three logical positions one can take concerning the prophetic claims of Joseph Smith.

First, *we can believe that Smith was whom he claimed to be*—God's latter-day prophet. This belief will lead us to accept his "restored gospel" and to become a member of his "true church" and, if a male, to seek to enter the priesthood reestablished through him. If he was whom he claimed to be, then every reasonable man or woman should become a follower of Joseph Smith.

Second, *we can believe that Smith was a fraud* and that he knowingly sought to deceive people in order to obtain their possessions and to control their lives. If Smith was a fraud and a liar, then he should be exposed and his religion should be ignored as an example of just another "Jim Jones" cult.

Third, *we can believe that Smith was insane* and that he had delusions of grandeur in which he thought he was a "prophet of God." In this light, he would be an object of pity. If he were alive today, he would be sent to a mental institution where those of like-claims can preach their delusions without being allowed to disturb the general public. Smith's sincerity, even unto death, would be viewed as another example of the multitudes of self-proclaimed false Christs and false prophets who have purposely martyred

24

themselves in order to "prove" their divine call.

Mormonism has its foundation and basis in the religious claims of Joseph Smith. Indeed, if Smith is a true prophet of God, then all pious people should seek to learn from the revelations he received. These revelations concerned the introduction of a "restored gospel," the setting up of a "true church" and the reestablishing of a "priesthood." Yet, the whole Mormon religion stands or falls on one issue: Was Joseph Smith a true prophet of God?

Since there are multitudes of people who have claimed to be a "prophet of God" and on the basis of that claim have demanded our obedience and devotion, we must be careful that we are not deceived. Indeed, Jesus Christ warned us in the Bible that false Christs and false prophets would seek to deceive us.

> Take heed that no man deceive you. For many shall come in my name, saying, I am Christ; and shall deceive many. . . . And many false prophets shall rise, and shall deceive many. . . . For there shall arise false Christs, and false prophets, and shall show great signs and wonders; insomuch that, if it were possible, they shall deceive the very elect. Behold, I have told you before. (Matt. 24:4-5, 11, 24-25)

Since there are false prophets who will seek to deceive us, we must have a sure way to detect a false prophet when we meet one. Is there a good way to test those who claim to be God's prophets?

> But the prophet, which shall presume to speak a word in my name, which I have not commanded him to speak, or that shall speak in the name of other gods, even that prophet shall die. And if thou say in thine heart, How shall we know the word which the Lord hath not spoken? When the prophet speaketh in the name of the Lord, if the thing follow not, nor come to pass, that is the thing which the Lord hath not spoken, but the prophet hath spoken it presumptuously: thou shalt not be afraid of him. (Deut. 18:20-22)

In the preceding passage, God gave Moses a sure way to detect a false prophet. If a person claims to be God's prophet but his prophecies (predictions) don't come to pass, that person is a false prophet. This is the simplest test possible, and it will work every time.

Joseph Smith claimed to be God's prophet. Therefore, the only way to test whether or not he was whom he claimed to be is to check his predictions to see if they were all fulfilled. Just one false prophecy would reveal that Smith was a false prophet, for God's prophets never give false prophecies.

We should also point out that Deut. 18:20-22 does not tell us to check our "feelings." The Bible points us to the *facts* of history to determine whether someone is a false prophet. We should not ask, "What do we feel about this person?", but we should ask, "What should we *think* about this person?"

The ultimate issue of Joseph Smith centers in historical records and events. Religious prejudice, belief, unbelief, or sincerity does not tell us anything, because every false prophet has his followers who "feel" that he is God's prophet. The facts of history and the primary documents must have the last say.

The following material is a collection of some of the predictions Joseph Smith made during his lifetime. Each prediction is found in authentic historic Mormon documents. In order to insure that no prediction or prophecy is taken out of context, the entire page from the primary source material is reproduced.

The reader has a responsibility to read each prophecy of Smith's in its context and then to decide on his own if it was or was not fulfilled. Questions are superimposed over the reproduced material to help the reader draw his conclusions. Let religious prejudice and bigotry be put aside and the historical documents speak for themselves.

This page is taken from a Mormon pamphlet entitled, *Joseph Smith—A Prophet of God.*

To Illinois they went, where in their distress, they were received kindly. At a desolate spot on the Mississippi they purchased a large tract of swamp land. This they drained, and here they built what became ~~~ largest city in Ill~~~

What is Joseph Smith remembered as? What is the foundation of the Mormon Church?

~~~ numbers, and ~~~pered for a season.

But the peace of Nauvoo was short-lived. Again bitter religious intolerance led to persecution. Joseph Smith and his brother Hyrum were imprisoned under false charges in Carthage, Illinois. There, while awaiting trial under the guaranteed protection of the state they were shot and killed June 27, 1844, by an armed mob with painted faces.

Brigham Young succeeded to the leadership of the Church. Under his direction the Latter-day Saints left Illinois and made their historic trek to the Rocky Mountains, where through struggle and faith they have become a mighty people.

By hundreds of thousands in many lands Joseph Smith is today held in remembrance as a prophet of God. The virtues and achievements of those who have accepted his testimony stand as a monument to his divine calling. The Church of Jesus Christ of Latter-day Saints has its foundation in the revelations he received, the sacred truths he taught, and the authority of the Priesthood restored through him.

coming from him, and it was the nature of the prophetic utterances which determined this division. Yet we have the word of the Lord definitely declaring to us that there was no greater prophet than John.[13]

By the same

According to Joseph Fielding Smith, a past president and prophet of the Mormon Church, upon whom does Mormonism stand or fall? According to him, what are the only two logical positions one can take concerning Smith? Is there any middle ground? If he is a fraud, what should we do? By what standard should we test Smith's claim? Is there salvation for those who reject Smith's claim?

powers and stands at the
... with all the authority that has been revealed and bestowed on man on the earth. Such a conclusion would certainly come out of a narrow construction and misunderstanding of the nature of the prophetic calling.[14]

THE DIVINE MISSION OF JOSEPH SMITH

CHURCH STANDS OR FALLS WITH JOSEPH SMITH. Mormonism, as it is called, must *stand or fall on the story of Joseph Smith*. He was either a prophet of God, divinely called, properly appointed and commissioned, or he was one of the biggest frauds this world has ever seen. *There is no middle ground.*[15]

If Joseph Smith was a deceiver, who wilfully attempted to mislead the people, then he should be exposed; his claims should be refuted, and his doctrines shown to be false, for the doctrines of an impostor cannot be made to harmonize in all particulars with divine truth. If his claims and declarations were built upon fraud and deceit, there would appear many errors and contradictions, which would be easy to detect. *The doctrines of false teachers will not stand the test when tried by the accepted standards of measurement, the scriptures.*[16]

[13]Luke 7:28; Matt. 3:2, 10-12.   [15]*Church News,* Apr. 1, 1939, p. 1.
[14]Pers. Corresp.   [16]*Millennial Star,* vol. 96, pp. 33-34.

ALL ATTACKS ON WORK OF JOSEPH SMITH FAIL.
There is no possibility of his being deceived, and on this
issue we are ready to make our stand. I maintain that
Joseph Smith was all that he claimed to be. His statements are too positive and his claims too great to admit
of deception on his part. No impostor could have accomplished so great and wonderful a work. Had he been
such, he would have been detected and exposed, and
the plan would have failed and come to naught.

In the plan of salvation, as it was made known
through Joseph Smith to the world, there are no flaws.
Each part fits perfectly and makes the whole complete.
Attacks have been made from the beginning to the present, and yet every one has failed. The world has been
unable to place a finger upon anything that is inconsistent,
or out of harmony in the revelations to Joseph Smith,
with that which has been revealed before, or predicted
by the prophets and the Lord himself.[17]

MAN CANNOT CREATE A PERFECT RELIGION. No
man, in and of himself, without the aid of the Spirit of
God and the direction of revelation, can found a religion,
or promulgate a body of doctrine, in all particulars in
harmony with revealed truth. If he has not the inspiration of the Lord and the direction of messengers from
his presence, he will not comprehend the truth, and therefore such truth as he teaches will be hopelessly mixed
with error. This is proved to be the case with many
professed founders of religious creeds. Their teachings
cannot be made to square themselves with the revelations
of Jesus Christ and his prophets.

NO SALVATION WITHOUT ACCEPTING JOSEPH
SMITH. If Joseph Smith was verily a prophet, and if he
told the truth when he said that he stood in the presence
of angels sent from the Lord, and obtained keys of
authority, and the commandment to organize the Church
of Jesus Christ once again on the earth, then this knowl-

[17]Conf. Rep., Apr., 1920, p. 106.

30

From the *Journal of Discourses*, Vol. 21

ages. Did they prosecute and persecute men in former ages? They did. Why? Was it because they were wicked and corrupt? No; it was because they dared to tell a corrupt world that God had spoken, that light and truth had been revealed from heaven, that the Son of God had ~~~~~~~~

they would pay no attention to you; they would look upon you as a very common-place, foolish individual, and morever, they would also look upon you as a fraud. Well, then, if God does not send men, of course they cannot act under the authority of God; if th~~ ~~~~

> If Smith was not a prophet of God, what is the only logical conclusion we can draw? Is there any middle ground?

~~~~ being the case, how then can they go forth in the name of God? I do not know; it is a mystery to me; these people possess some mysteries which I cannot fathom, and that is one of them. I know of only three ways of obtaining authority of that kind —one is by lineal descent, another by writing, and a third by speaking. Now, then, if we can find no record among the people who profess to teach in the name of God, and they do not profess to have a lineal descent, and they even hold that God has not spoken for eighteen hundred years —they place themselves in a very awkward position. But when you come to understand, to fully comprehend the priesthood held by our forefathers, you can see by what authority the Holy priesthood is conferred upon you. Well, then, where did you get this authority from—from the world? No, the world did not have it to give, and consequently you could not get it from them; and if God has not spoken, if the angel of God has not appeared to Joseph Smith, and if these things are not true of which we speak, then the whole thing is an imposture from beginning to end. There is no half-way house, no middle path about the matter; it is either one thing or the other. Now you go forth to the nations of the

~~~ ~~~ doctrine they taught; that is the doctrine that we teach. Is there anything very remarkable about it? Yes, very remarkable. Is there a people that dare say what the Elders of the Latter-day Saints dare say to the world? I think not. What have these elders done, many of whom are here? Gone to the ends of the earth without purse or scrip proclaiming the Gospel of the Son of God. And what did they tell the people to do? To repent and be baptized for the remission of their sins and to have hands laid upon them for the reception of the Holy Ghost; and you do the same; you baptize them when they believe in the name of the Father, and of the Son and of the Holy Ghost. And what does a name mean? Power and authority. Supposing a man was to come here as Governor or Secretary, or holding any other office under the government of the United States; he comes in the name of the United States, or by the power or authority of the United States, does he not? Yes. But supposing some of you was to set up here as Governor, they would want to see your credentials and know by what authority you came here and whether you were appointed by the legitimate authorities of the United States or not. If not,

1. JOSEPH SMITH AND THE RETURN OF CHRIST

In the early 1800s there arose a flurry of predictions concerning the return of Christ. The Rev. William Miller, founder of the Adventist Church, predicted that Christ must come no later than 1843. Much excitement was generated as that date approached.

Joseph Smith frequently spoke concerning the Second Coming of Christ. He described with great detail all the judgments which would precede the day of Christ's return. With Miller's prediction approaching, Smith spoke directly concerning "father Miller's" date in order to calm the saints.

It is important to check the historic documents to see if Smith believed and prophesied that Christ would return in his own generation. Did he teach that it was about to occur in his own day? Did he give a date for Christ's return? What did the Mormons who lived during this time believe? What did they hear Joseph Smith teach concerning the Second Coming of Christ? Only the historic documents can give us the answers. We must let the documents speak for themselves.

his legs, a little above the ankles. His head and neck were also bare. I could discover that he had no other clothing on but this robe, as it was open, so that I could see into his bosom.

32. Not only was his robe exceedingly white, but his whole person was glorious beyond description, and his countenance truly like lightning. The room was exceedingly light, but not so very bright as immediately …

According to Smith, when was Joel 2:28-32 to be fulfilled? When would the fullness of the Gentiles come in? What generation would experience these things? Since all these predictions failed, what kind of a prophet does Smith appear to be?

… for good and evil among all nations, kindreds, and tongues, or that it should be both good and evil spoken of among all people.

34. He said there was a book deposited, written upon gold plates, giving an account of the former inhabitants of this continent, and the source from whence they sprang. He also said that the fulness of the everlasting Gospel was contained in it, as delivered by the Savior to the ancient inhabitants;

35. Also, that there were two stones in silver bows—and these stones, fastened to a breastplate, constituted what is called the Urim and Thummim—deposited with the plates; and the possession and use of these stones were what constituted "seers" in ancient or former times; and that God had prepared them for the purpose of translating the book.

36. After telling me these things, he commenced quoting the prophecies of the Old Testament. He first quoted part of the third chapter of Malachi; and he quoted also the fourth or last chapter of the same prophecy, though with a little variation from the way it reads in our Bibles. Instead of quoting the first verse as it reads in our books, he quoted it thus:

37. *For behold, the day cometh that shall burn as …* … *Elijah the prophet, before the coming of the great and dreadful day of the Lord.*

39. He also quoted the next verse differently: *And he shall plant in the hearts of the children the promises made to the fathers, and the hearts of the children shall turn to their fathers. If it were not so, the whole earth would be utterly wasted at his coming.*

40. In addition to these, he quoted the eleventh chapter of Isaiah, saying that it was about to be fulfilled. He quoted also the third chapter of Acts, twenty-second and twenty-third verses, precisely as they stand in our New Testament. He said that that prophet was Christ; but the day had not yet come when "they who would not hear his voice should be cut off from among the people," but soon would come.

41. He also quoted the second chapter of Joel, from the twenty-eighth verse to the last. He also said that this was not yet fulfilled, but was soon to be. And he further stated that the fulness of the Gentiles was soon to come

in. He quoted many other passages of scripture, and offered many explanations which cannot be mentioned here.

42. Again, he told me, that when I got those plates of which he had spoken—for the time that they should be obtained was not yet fulfilled—I should not show them to any person; neither the breastplate with the Urim and Thummim; only to those to whom I should be commanded to show them; if I did I should be destroyed. While he was conversing with me about the plates, the vision was opened to my mind that I could see the place where the plates were deposited, and that so clearly and distinctly that I knew the place again when I visited it.

43. After this communication, I saw the light in the room begin to gather immediately around the person of him who had been speaking to me, and it continued to do so until the room was again left dark, except just around him; when, instantly I saw, as it were, a conduit open right up into heaven, and he ascended till he entirely disappeared, and the room was left as it had been before this heavenly light had made its appearance.

44. I lay musing on the singularity of the scene, and marveling greatly at what had been told to me by this extraordinary messenger; when, in the midst of my meditation, I suddenly discovered that my room was again beginning to get lighted, and in an instant, as it were, the same heavenly messenger was again by my bedside.

45. He commenced, and again related the very same things which he had done at his first visit, without the least variation; which having done, <u>he informed me of great judgments which were coming upon the earth, with great desolations by famine</u>, <u>sword, and pestilence; and that these grievous judgments would come on the earth in this generation.</u> Having related these things, he again ascended as he had done before.

46. By this time, so deep were the impressions made on my mind, that sleep had fled from my eyes, and I lay overwhelmed in astonishment at what I had both seen and heard. But what was my surprise when again I beheld the same messenger at my bedside, and heard him rehearse or repeat over again to me the same things as before; and added a caution to me, telling me that Satan would try to tempt me (in consequence of the indigent circumstances of my father's family), to get the plates for the purpose of getting rich. This he forbade me, saying that I must have no other object in view in getting the plates but to glorify God, and must not be influenced by any other motive than that of building his kingdom; otherwise I could not get them.

47. After this third visit, he again ascended into heaven as before, and I was again left to ponder on the strangeness of what I had just experienced; when almost immediately after the heavenly messenger had ascended from me for the third time, the cock crowed, and I found that day was approaching, so that our interviews must have occupied the whole of that night.

48. I shortly after arose from my bed, and, as usual, went to the necessary labors of the day; but, in attempting to work as at other times, I found my strength

him and thee alone, and tell him that those things which he hath written from that stone are not of me, and that Satan °deceiveth him;

12. For, behold, these things have not been appointed unto him, neither shall anything be appointed unto any of this church contrary to the church covenants.

13. For all things must be done in order, and by 'common consent in the °church, by the prayer of faith.

14. And thou shalt assist to settle all these things, according to the covenants of the church, before thou shalt take thy journey among the Lamanites.

15. And it shall be given thee from the time thou shalt go, until the time thou shalt return, what thou shalt do.

16. And thou must open thy mouth at all times, declaring my gospel with the sound of rejoicing. Amen.

SECTION 29.

REVELATION *given through Joseph Smith the Prophet, in the presence of six Elders, at Fayette, New York, September, 1830. This revelation was given some days prior to the conference beginning September 26, 1830. —— The gathering of the elect specified—The imminence of the Lord's advent affirmed—Calamities incident to the sinful state of the world—The Millennium and scenes of judgment to follow—Distinction between the spiritual and temporal creations—Purpose of the mortal probation—The agency of man—The assured redemption of children who die in infancy.*

1. Listen to the voice of Jesus Christ, your Red...

In 1830, what did Smith affirm? When would the earth be ripe? When would the wicked be burned up? Did it happen? Smith's prediction in 1830 that the hour of judgment was "nigh," "soon," "at hand," etc., reveals that he expected Christ to return during his lifetime. This, of course, did not take place.

...you, therefore ye receive these things; but remember to sin no more, lest perils shall come upon you.

4. Verily, I say unto you that ye are chosen out of the world to declare my gospel with the sound of rejoicing, ᵇas with the voice of a trump.

5. Lift up your hearts and be

...and Fa-to

...h, ...ng e. g e y

...on hearts; ...therefore the decree hath gone forth from the Father that they shall be gathered in unto ᵒone place upon the face of this land, to prepare their hearts and be prepared in all things against the day when ʲtribulation and desolation are sent forth upon the wicked.

9. For the ᵖhour is nigh and the day soon at hand when the

e, 43:5—7.   49:23.   f, see 2u, sec. 20.   g, see a, sec. 1.   SEC. 29: a, ver. 8. See j, sec. 10.   b, 19:37.   30:9.   33:2.   34:6.   36:1.   42:6.   75:4.   124:7. Isa. 58:1. c, see c, sec. 4.   d, see j, sec. 10.   e, see d.   f, see f and g, sec. 1.   g, see b, sec. 4.

earth is ripe; and all the proud and they that do wickedly shall be as stubble; and I will [a]burn them up, saith the Lord of Hosts, that wickedness shall not be upon the earth;

10. For the hour is nigh, and that which was spoken by mine apostles must be fulfilled; for as they spoke so shall it come to pass;

11. For I will reveal [i]myself from heaven with power and great glory, with all the hosts thereof, and dwell in righteousness with men on earth a [j]thousand years, and the wicked shall not stand.

12. And again, verily, verily, I say unto you, and it hath gone forth in a firm decree, by the will of the Father, that mine apostles, the Twelve which were with me in my ministry at Jerusalem, shall stand at my right hand at the day of my coming in a pillar of fire, being clothed with robes of righteousness, with [k]crowns upon their heads, in glory even as I am, to judge the whole house of Israel, even as many as have loved me and kept my commandments, and none else.

13. For a [l]trump shall sound both long and loud, even as upon Mount Sinai, and all the earth shall quake, and they shall come forth—yea, [m]even the dead which died in me, to receive a crown of righteousness, and to be clothed upon, even as I am, to be with me, that we may be one.

14. But, behold, I say unto you that before this great day shall come the [n]sun shall be darkened, and the moon shall be turned into blood, and the stars shall fall from heaven, and there shall be greater signs in heaven above and in the earth beneath;

15. And there shall be [o]weeping and wailing among the hosts of men;

16. And there shall be a [p]great hailstorm sent forth to destroy the crops of the earth.

17. And it shall come to pass, because of the wickedness of the world, that I will take [q]vengeance upon the wicked, for they will not repent; for the cup of mine indignation is full; for behold, my blood shall not cleanse them if they hear me not.

18. Wherefore, I the Lord God will send forth [r]flies upon the face of the earth, which shall take hold of the inhabitants thereof, and shall eat their flesh, and shall cause maggots to come in upon them;

19. And their tongues shall be stayed that they shall not utter against me; and their flesh shall fall from off their bones, and their eyes from their sockets;

20. And it shall come to pass that the [s]beasts of the forest and the fowls of the air shall devour them up.

21. And the great and [t]abominable church, which is the whore of all the earth, shall be cast down by devouring fire, according as it is spoken by the mouth of Ezekiel the prophet, who spoke of these things, which have not come to pass but surely must, as

h, see i, sec. 1.   i, see e, sec. 1.   j, ver. 22. See e, sec. 1.   43:30. Rev. 20:4—6.   k, Matt. 19:28. Luke 22:30. l Ne. 12:9.   l, 29:13. 43:18. 45:45. 49:23. 88:98, 99.   m, 45:45, 46. 76:50—64. 88:14—17, 20, 27—29, 96, 97. 133:56. Dan. 12:2, 3. Luke 14:14. Acts 24:15. Rev. 20:5, 6. Mos. 15:8, 9, 20—27. 16:7— 11. Al. chap. 40. 42:23. He. 14:15—17, 25. 3 Ne. 26:5. Morm. 7:6. 9:13. n, 34:9. 45:42. 88:87. 133:49. Isa. 13:6—13. Joel 2:31. Matt. 24:29. Rev. 6:12—17. o, see e, sec. 19. p, 43:25. 63:6. 88:89, 90. 109:30. Isa. 28:17. Ezek. 38:22. Rev. 8:7. q, see f and g, sec 1. r, Ex. 8:21. Zech. 14:12. Isa. 18:6. s, Isa. 18:6. Ezek. 39:17—20. Rev. 19:17, 18.   t, see j, sec. 18. Ezek. 38:22.

36

The Lord hath gathered "all things in one.

The Lord hath brought down "Zion from above.

The Lord hath brought up "Zion from beneath.

101. The earth hath travailed and brought forth her strength;

And truth is established in her bowels;

And the heavens have smiled upon her:

And ...

For ...

1(...

Be a ...

Justi ... truth, and

Forever and ever, Amen.

103. And again, verily, verily I say unto you, it is expedient that every man who goes forth to proclaim mine everlasting gospel, that inasmuch as they have families, and receive money by gift, that they should send it unto them or make use of it for their benefit, as the Lord shall direct them, for thus it seemeth me good.

104. And let all those who have not families, who receive money, send it up unto the bishop in Zion, or unto the bishop in Ohio, that it may be consecrated for the bringing forth of the revelations and the printing thereof, and for establishing Zion.

105. And if any man shall give unto any of you a coat, or a suit, take the old and cast it unto the poor, and go on your way rejoicing.

106. And if any man among

you be strong in the Spirit, let him take with him him that is weak, that he may be edified in all meekness, that he may become strong also.

107. Therefore, take with you those who are ordained unto the "lesser priesthood, and send them before you to make appointments, and to prepare the way, and to fill appo... ... ou

... the feet it ... no need of the feet; for without the feet how shall the body be able to stand?

110. Also the body hath need of every member, that all may be edified together, that the system may be kept perfect.

111. And behold, the "high priests should travel, and also the elders, and also the lesser priests; but the deacons and teachers should be appointed to watch over the church, to be standing ministers unto the church.

112. And the bishop, Newel K. Whitney, also should travel round about and among all the churches, searching after the poor to administer to their wants by humbling the rich and the proud.

113. He should also employ an agent to take charge and to do his secular business as he shall direct.

114. Nevertheless, let the bishop go unto the city of New York, also to the city of Albany, and also to the city of Boston, and warn the people of those cities

> Why were the people of New York, Albany, and Boston to listen? When would their hour of judgment come? Did these things happen? Since these cities were never destroyed by divine judgment, what should we conclude about Smith's prophecy?

4e, see j, sec 10.　4f, 45:11—14.　P. of G. P., Moses 7:62—64.　4g. see 31, sec. 76.　4h, Isa. 11:9.　4i, see a, sec. 13.　4j, 1 Cor. 12:21.　4k, see i, sec. 68.

with the sound of the gospel, with a loud voice, of the [4l]desolation and utter abolishment which await them if they do reject these things.

115. For if they do reject these things the hour of their judgment is nigh, and their house shall be left unto them desolate.

116. Let him trust in me and he shall not be confounded; and a hair of his head shall not fall to the ground unnoticed.

117. And verily I say unto you, the rest of my servants, go ye forth as your circumstances shall permit, in your several callings, unto the great and notable cities and villages, reproving the world in righteousness of all their [4m]un-righteous and ungodly deeds, setting forth clearly and understandingly the [4n]desolation of abomination in the last days.

118. For, with you saith the Lord Almighty, I will [4o]rend their kingdoms; I will not only [4p]shake the earth, but the [4q]starry heavens shall tremble.

119. For I, the Lord, have put forth my hand to [4r]exert the powers of heaven; ye cannot see it now, yet a little while and ye shall see it, and know that I am, and that I will [4s]come and reign with my people.

120. I am Alpha and Omega, the beginning and the end. Amen.

SECTION 85.

REVELATION *given through Joseph Smith the Prophet, at Kirtland, Ohio, November 27, 1832, concerning the Saints in Zion, Missouri. See History of the Church, vol. 1, p. 298.* —— *Inheritances in Zion to be received through consecration—Provision made for the assignment of inheritances among the Saints.*

1. It is the duty of the Lord's clerk, whom he has appointed, to keep a [a]history, and a general church record of all things that transpire in Zion, and of all those who consecrate properties, and receive inheritances legally from the bishop;

2. And also their manner of life, their faith, and works; and also of the apostates who apostatize after receiving their inheritances.

3. It is contrary to the will and commandment of God that those who receive not their inheritance by [b]consecration, agreeable to his law, which he has given, that he may tithe his people, to prepare them against the day of [c]vengeance and burning, should have their names enrolled with the people of God.

4. Neither is their [d]genealogy to be kept, or to be had where it may be found on any of the records or history of the church.

5. Their names shall not be found, neither the names of the fathers, nor the names of the children written in the [e]book of the law of God, saith the Lord of Hosts.

6. Yea, thus saith the [f]still small voice, which whispereth through and pierceth all things,

4l, see f and g, sec. 1.   4m, ver. 87.   4n, see f and g, sec. 1.   4o, Dan. 2:34, 35, 44, 45.   4p, see e, sec. 21.   4q, see e, sec. 21.   4r, see e, sec. 21. 4s, see e, sec. 1.   Sec. 85:   a, see a, sec. 21.   b, see n, sec. 42.   c, see f and g, sec. 1.   d, Ezra 2:62, 63.   e, vers. 1, 9.   f, 1 Kings 19:11—13.

God, until the ʳconsumption decreed hath made a full end of all nations;

7. That the cry of the saints, and of the ʲblood of the saints, shall cease to come up into the ears of the Lord of Sabaoth, from the earth, to be avenged of their enemies.

8. Wherefore, stand ye in ⁹holy places, and be not moved, until the ʰday of the Lord come; for behold, it cometh quickly, saith the Lord. Amen.

SECTION 88.

REVELATION *given through Joseph Smith the Prophet, at Kirtland, Ohio, December 27, 1832.* *Designated by the Prophet, the Olive Leaf. See History of the Church, v.. 1. p. 302.* —— *Ministrations of the Comforter—The light of truth is the light of Christ—The spirit and the body constitute the soul—Parable of the man sending his servants into the field and visiting them in turn—Search for the truth through study and prayer enjoined—Testimony of the Elders to be followed by that of calamity—Scenes incident to the Lord's coming—The angels sounding their trumpets in turn as appointed—Duties of the Presidency of the School of the Prophets—The ordinance of washing of feet.*

1. Verily, thus saith the L... unto you ...

When did Smith say that the earth would reel and the sun would hide its face? For what should the people of his generation prepare? Did his generation see these things fulfilled? Since in 1832 Smith predicted that these things would happen in "not many days hence," we must conclude over 150 years later, that Smith's prophecy was false.

... and through all ... "the light of truth;

7. Which truth shineth. This is the light of Christ. As also he is ʳin the sun, and the light of the sun, and the power thereof by which it was made.

3. ... you ... Comforter, even upon you my friends, that it may abide in your hearts, even the Holy Spirit of promise; which other Comforter is the same that I promised unto my disciples, as is recorded in the testimony of John.

4. This Comforter is the promise which I give unto you of eter-

8. As also he is in the ʲmoon, and is the light of the moon, and the power thereof by which it was made;

9. As also the ⁹light of the

e, see f and g, sec 1.   f, 58:53.   63:28—31.   1 Ne. 14:13.   22:14.   2 Ne.
27:2, 3.   28:10.   Morm. 8:27, 40, 41.   Eth. 8:22—24.   Rev. 6:9, 10.   18:24.   19:2.
g, 45:32.   101:64.   h, see e, sec. 1, and b, sec. 2.   SEC. 88:   a, vers. 4, 5.   See
h. sec. 42.   b, see a, sec. 1.   c, 122:8.   Eph. 4:9, 10.   d, vers. 7—13, 40, 41,
49. 50, 66, 67.   14:9.   84:44—48.   93:2, 8—17, 26, 23—39.   e, see d.   f, see d.
g. see d.

80. That ye may be prepared in all things when I shall send you again to magnify the calling whereunto I have called you, and the mission with which I have commissioned you.

81. Behold, I sent you out to testify and warn the people, and it becometh every man who hath been warned to warn his neighbor.

82. Therefore, they are left without excuse, and their sins are upon their own heads.

83. He that seeketh me early shall find me, and shall not be forsaken.

84. Therefore, tarry ye, and labor diligently, that you may be perfected in your ministry to go forth among the Gentiles for the last time, as many as the mouth of the Lord shall name, to ¹ᵛbind up the law and seal up the testimony, and to prepare the saints for the hour of judgment which is to come;

85. That their souls may escape the wrath of God, the ¹ʷdesolation of abomination which awaits the wicked, both in this world and in the world to come. Verily, I say unto you, let those who are not the first elders continue in the vineyard until the mouth of the Lord shall call them, for their time is not yet come; their garments are not clean from the blood of this generation.

86. Abide ye in the liberty wherewith ye are made free; entangle not yourselves in sin, but let your hands be clean, until the Lord comes.

87. For not many days hence and the earth shall tremble and ²ˣreel to and fro as a drunken man; and the sun shall ²ʸhide his face, and shall refuse to give light; and the moon shall be bathed in blood; and the stars shall become exceedingly angry, and shall cast themselves down as a fig that falleth from off a fig-tree.

88. And after your testimony cometh wrath and indignation upon the people.

89. For after your testimony cometh the ²ᶻtestimony of earthquakes, that shall cause groanings in the midst of her, and men shall fall upon the ground and shall not be able to stand.

90. And also cometh the testimony of the voice of thunderings, and the voice of lightnings, and the voice of tempests, and the voice of the waves of the sea heaving themselves beyond their bounds.

91. And all things shall be in commotion; and surely, men's hearts shall fail them; for fear shall come upon all people.

92. And angels shall fly through the midst of heaven, crying with a ³ᵃloud voice, sounding the trump of God, saying: Prepare ye, prepare ye, O inhabitants of the earth; for the judgment of our God is come. Behold, and lo, the Bridegroom cometh; go ye out to meet him.

93. And immediately there shall appear a ³ᵇgreat sign in heaven, and all people shall see it together.

94. And another angel shall sound his trump, saying: That ³ᶜgreat church, the mother of abominations, that made all nations drink of the wine of the wrath of her fornication, that persecuteth the saints of God,

---

2v, see d, sec. 1. Isa. 8:16. 2w, 84:114, 117. Dan. 9:27. 12:11. Matt. 24:15. 2x, see x, sec. 45. 2y, see n, sec. 29. 2z, see x, sec. 45. 3a, 43:18, 25. 20:6. 128:19—21. 133:17. Testimony of Three Witnesses, Book of Mormon. 3b, Luke 21:25—27. 3c, 29:21.

chosen to bear testimony of my name and to *send it abroad among all nations, kindreds, tongues, and people, and ordained through the instrumentality of my servants.

2. Verily I say unto you, there have been some few things in thine heart and with thee with which I, the Lord, was not well pleased.

3. Nevertheless, inasmuch as thou hast abased th—— ——— shalt be ex——— th—

c. —— sl— n— al— sh— the ——

5 — mo— afte— go 1 ——— —— voice cometh let not the inhabitants of the earth slumber, because of thy speech.

6. Let thy habitation be known in Zion, and remove not thy house; for I, the Lord, have a great work for thee to do, in publishing my name among the children of men.

7. Therefore, gird up thy loins for the work. Let thy feet be shod also, for thou art chosen, and thy path lieth among the mountains, and among many nations.

8. And by thy word many high ones shall be brought low, and by thy word many low ones shall be exalted.

9. Thy voice shall be a rebuke unto the transgressor; and at thy rebuke let the tongue of the slanderer cease its perverseness.

10. Be thou humble; and the

Lord thy God shall lead thee by the hand, and give thee answer to thy prayers.

11. I know thy heart, and have heard thy prayers concerning thy brethren. Be not partial towards them in love above many others, but let thy love be for them as for thyself; and let thy love abound unto all men, and ——— —— who love my na—

—— ——— —— ——— ——— not their ———ted, and I will heal them.

14. Now, I say unto you, and what I say unto you, I say unto all the ᵇTwelve: Arise and gird up your loins, take up your cross, follow me, and feed my sheep.

15. Exalt not yourselves; rebel not against my servant Joseph; for verily I say unto you, I am with him, and my hand shall be over him; and the ᶜkeys which I have given unto him, and also to youward, shall not be taken from him till I come.

16. Verily I say unto you, my servant Thomas, thou art the man whom I have chosen to hold the keys of my kingdom, as pertaining to the Twelve, abroad among all nations—

17. That thou mayest be my servant to unlock the door of the kingdom in all places where my servant Joseph, and my servant Sidney, and my servant Hyrum, cannot come;

18. For on them have I laid

How long would Smith be active in using the keys given to him? Since he must be alive to use the keys, does this passage indicate that Smith would be alive on earth when Christ returned? Since the words "till I come" can only refer to the Second Coming, Smith's prophecy must be assumed to be wrong.

a, see q, sec. 18.   b, Matt. 16:24.   John 21:15—17.   c, see b, sec. 28.

the burden of all the churches for a little season.

19. Wherefore, whithersoever they shall send you, go ye, and I will be with you; and in whatsoever place ye shall proclaim my name an effectual door shall be opened unto you, that they may receive my word.

20. Whosoever receiveth my word receiveth me, and whosoever receiveth me, receiveth those, the First Presidency, whom I have sent, whom I have made counselors for my name's sake unto you.

21. And again, I say unto you, that whosoever ye shall send in my name, by the voice of your brethren, the Twelve, duly recommended and authorized by you, shall have *power to open the door of my kingdom unto any nation whithersoever ye shall send them—

22. Inasmuch as they shall humble themselves before me, and abide in my word, and hearken to the voice of my Spirit.

23. Verily, verily, I say unto you, *darkness covereth the earth, and gross darkness the minds of the people, and *all flesh has become corrupt before my face.

24. Behold, *vengeance cometh speedily upon the inhabitants of the earth, a day of wrath, a day of burning, a day of desolation, of weeping, of mourning, and of lamentation; and as a whirlwind it shall come upon all the face of the earth, saith the Lord.

25. And upon my house *shall it begin, and from my house shall it go forth, saith the Lord;

26. First among those among you, saith the Lord, who have professed to know my name and have not known me, and have blasphemed against me in the midst of my house, saith the Lord.

27. Therefore, see to it that ye trouble not yourselves concerning the affairs of my church in this place, saith the Lord.

28. But purify your hearts before me; and then 'go ye into all the world, and preach my gospel unto every creature who has not received it;

29. And 'he that believeth and is baptized shall be saved, and he that believeth not, and is not baptized, shall be damned.

30. For unto you, the Twelve, and those, the First Presidency, who are appointed with you to be your counselors and your leaders, is the power of this priesthood given, for the last days and for the last time, in the which is the *dispensation of the fulness of times.

31. Which power you hold, in connection with all those who have received a dispensation at any time from the beginning of the creation;

32. For verily I say unto you, the 'keys of the dispensation, which ye have received, have come down from the fathers, and last of all, being sent down from heaven unto you.

33. Verily I say unto you, behold how great is your calling. Cleanse your hearts and your garments, lest the blood of this generation be required at your hands.

34. Be faithful until I come, for I *come quickly; and my reward is with me to recompense every man according as his work shall be. I am Alpha and Omega. Amen.

d, 107:34, 35, 38, 95—98.   e, Isa. 60:2.   f, 38:10—12.   g, see f and g. sec. 1.   h, 1 Pet. 4:17, 18.   i, see q, sec. 18.   j, see q, sec. 20.   k, see n, sec. 27.   l, see k, sec. 6.   m, see e, sec. 1.

Verily, thus saith the Lord, the time is now come, that it shall be disposed of by a council, composed of the First Presidency of my Church, and of the bishop and his council, and by my high council; and by mine own voice unto them, saith the Lord. Even so. Amen.

SECTION 121.

PRAYER AND PROPHECIES, *written by Joseph Smith the Prophet, while a prisoner in the jail at Liberty, Missouri, dated March 20, 1839. The Prophet with several companions had been months in prison. Their petitions and appeals directed to the executive officers and the judiciary had failed to bring them relief. See History of the Church, vol. 3, p. 289. —— Fervent appeals to the Lord in behalf of the suffering Saints—The curse of the Lord to fall upon those wh-   tend against his will—Men though called may not h* *   ts of the Priesthood inseparably conn   Un- righteous exercis*   y— Po*   *

Was the destruction of Smith's enemies far off or near? Did Smith believe that his generation would witness the judgments of the last times? Since Smith's enemies and their posterity were never "swept" away by divine judgment, what should we conclude about this prophecy?

A   rd co   ed sta   ie pu   *   thy hea   us of our wrongs. ple   * Remember thy suffering ear   * ated with their saints, O our God; and thy serv- cries: ants will rejoice in thy name forever.

3. Yea, O Lord, how long shall they suffer these wrongs and unlawful oppressions, before thine heart shall be softened toward them, and thy bowels be moved with compassion toward them?

4. O Lord God Almighty, maker of heaven, earth, and seas, and of all things that in them are, and who controllest and subjectest the devil, and the dark and benighted dominion of Sheol— stretch forth thy hand; let thine eye pierce; let thy pavilion be taken up; let thy hiding place no longer be covered; let thine ear be inclined; let thine heart be softened, and thy bowels

7. My son, peace be unto thy soul; thine adversity and thine afflictions shall be but a small moment;

8. And then, if thou endure it well, God shall exalt thee on high; thou shalt triumph over all thy foes.

9. Thy friends do stand by thee, and they shall hail thee again with warm hearts and friendly hands.

10. Thou art not yet as Job; thy friends do not contend against thee, neither charge thee with transgression, as they did Job.

11. And they who do charge thee with transgression, their

a, see 3j, sec. 101.   *b*, see 3j, sec. 101.   *c*, see f and g, sec. 1.

hope shall be blasted, and their prospects shall melt away as the hoar frost melteth before the burning rays of the rising sun;

12. And also that God hath set his hand and seal to change the times and seasons, and to blind their minds, that they may not understand *his marvelous workings; that he may prove them also and take them in their own craftiness;

13. Also because their hearts are corrupted, and the things which they are willing to bring upon others, and love to have others suffer, may come upon themselves to the very uttermost;

14. That they may be disappointed also, and their hopes may be cut off;

15. And not many years hence, that they and their posterity shall be 'swept from under heaven, saith God, that not one of them is left to stand by the wall.

16. Cursed are all those that shall lift up the heel against 'mine anointed, saith the Lord, and cry they have sinned when they have not sinned before me, saith the Lord, but have done that which was meet in mine eyes, and which I commanded them.

17. But those who cry transgression do it because they are the servants of sin, and are the children of disobedience themselves.

18. And those who swear falsely against my servants, that they might bring them into bondage and death—

19. Wo unto them; because they have offended my little ones they shall be severed from the ordinances of mine house.

20. Their basket shall not be full, their houses and their barns shall perish, and they themselves shall be despised by those that flattered them.

21. They shall not have right to the priesthood, nor their posterity after them from generation to generation.

22. It had been better for them that a millstone had been hanged about their necks, and they drowned in the depth of the sea.

23. Wo unto all those that discomfort my people, and drive, and murder, and testify against them, saith the Lord of Hosts; a generation of vipers shall not escape the damnation of hell.

24. Behold, mine eyes see and know all their works, and I have in reserve a swift judgment in the season thereof, for them all;

25. For there is a time appointed for every man, according as his works shall be.

26. God shall give unto you *knowledge by his Holy Spirit, yea, by the unspeakable gift of the Holy Ghost, that has not been revealed since the world was until now;

27. Which our forefathers have awaited with anxious expectation to be revealed in the last times, which their minds were pointed to by the angels, as *held in reserve for the fulness of their glory;

28. A time to come in the which nothing shall be withheld, whether there be one God or *many gods, they shall be manifest.

29. All thrones and dominions, principalities and powers, shall be revealed and set forth upon 'all who have endured valiantly for the gospel of Jesus Christ.

d, see a, sec. 4.   e, 41:1.   f, 132:7.   g, see 2e, sec. 42.   h, see 2e, sec. 42.   i, 76:58.   132:20.   j, see 2y, sec. 76, and 2b, sec. 101.

in his glory; for that is the only way he can appear—

7. Ask him to shake hands with you, but he will not move, because it is contrary to the order of heaven for a just man to deceive; but he will still deliver his message.

8. If it be the devil as an angel of light, when you ask him to shake hands he will offer you his hand, and you will not feel anything; you may therefore detect him.

9. These are 'three grand keys whereby you may know whether any administration is from God.

SECTION 130.

IMPORTANT ITEMS OF INSTRUCTION *given by Joseph Smith the Prophet, at Ramus, Illinois, April 2, 1843.* —— *When the Savior appears he will be in his true form, that of a man—The abode of the angels—The earth in its sanctified and immortalized condition—Prophecy of great difficulties involving much bloodshed to begin in South Carolina—Time of the Lord's coming not definitely made known— Intelligence acquired in this life will abide with its possessor—The law decreed in heaven, that blessings are obtained only by obedience to the laws upon which they are predicated—The Father and the Son possess bodies of flesh and bones—The Holy Ghost a person* ~~~

1. When the Savior sh[all] ... pear we shall ...

[overlaid annotation:] In verse 12, was Smith giving a prophecy? This prophecy concerned the coming of whom? What was to happen just before the Second Coming of Jesus Christ? In verse 14, what did Smith want to know? In verse 15, what did Jesus supposedly tell him? In verse 17, what did Smith conclude? The bloodshed in South Carolina did not lead to the coming of Christ (v. 12), and Christ did not come in 1890 (when Smith would have been 85).

4. ... question—

Is ... reckoning of God's time, angel's time, prophet's time, and man's time, according to the planet on which they reside?

5. I answer, Yes. But there are no angels who minister to this earth but those who do belong or have belonged to it.

... be a ...mmim to the inhabitants who dwell thereon, whereby all things pertaining to an inferior kingdom, or all kingdoms of a lower order, will be manifest to those who dwell on it; and this earth will be Christ's.

10. Then the white stone mentioned in Revelation 2:17, will become a Urim and Thummim to each individual who receives one,

c, vers. 1—8.

45

whereby things pertaining to a higher order of kingdoms will be made known;

11. And a white stone is given to each of those who come into the celestial kingdom, whereon is a new name written, which no man knoweth save he that receiveth it. The new name is the key word.

12. I prophesy, in the name of the Lord God, that the commencement of the difficulties which will cause much bloodshed previous to the coming of the Son of Man will be in South Carolina.

13. It may probably arise through the slave question. This a voice declared to me, while I was praying earnestly on the subject, December 25th, 1832.

14. I was once praying very earnestly to know the time of the coming of the Son of Man, when I heard a voice repeat the following:

15. Joseph, my son, if thou livest until thou art eighty-five years old, thou shalt see the face of the Son of Man; therefore let this suffice, and trouble me no more on this matter.

16. I was left thus, without being able to decide whether this coming referred to the beginning of the millennium or to some previous appearing, or whether I should die and thus see his face.

17. I believe the coming of the Son of Man will not be any sooner than that time. (1890)

18. Whatever principle of intelligence we attain unto in this life, it will rise with us in the resurrection.

19. And if a person gains more knowledge and intelligence in this life through his diligence and obedience than another, he will have so much the advantage in the world to come.

20. There is a law, irrevocably decreed in heaven before the foundations of this world, upon which all blessings are predicated—

21. And when we obtain any blessing from God, it is by obedience to that law upon which it is predicated.

22. The Father has a body of flesh and bones as tangible as man's; the Son also; but the Holy Ghost has not a body of flesh and bones, but is a personage of Spirit. Were it not so, the Holy Ghost could not dwell in us.

23. A man may receive the Holy Ghost, and it may descend upon him and not tarry with him.

SECTION 131.

INSTRUCTIONS *by Joseph Smith the Prophet, given at Ramus, Illinois, May 16 and 17, 1843. See History of the Church, vol. 5, pp. 392, 393.* —— *Degrees in the celestial glory—Significance of the new and everlasting covenant of marriage—The more sure word of prophecy—Impossibility of a man being saved in ignorance—Spirit is matter.*

1. In the celestial glory there are ªthree heavens or degrees;

2. And in order to obtain the highest, a man must enter into this ᵇorder of the priesthood [meaning the new and everlasting covenant of marriage];

3. And if he does not, he cannot obtain it.

4. He may enter into the other,

a, 2 Cor. 12:1—4.   b, 132:6—21.

thority of the Melchizedek Priesthood was manifested and conferred for the first time upon several of the Elders.* It was clearly evident that the Lord gave us power in proportion to the work to be done, and strength according to the race set before us, and grace and help as our needs required.† Great harmony prevailed; several were ordained; faith was strengthened;

* A misapprehension has arisen in the minds of --
"The authority of the Melchizedek P-
the first time upon sever-'
meant that --'

In 1831, when Smith ordained Lyman Wight, what did Lyman prophesy concerning his generation and the Second Coming of Christ? Did Smith object to Wight's teaching? This tells us that Smith and the early Mormons believed Christ would come in their own generation.

_____ ar as Apostles
_____ iv: 63); and of course as
_____ to the apostleship before this conference of
_____ there had been High Priests in the Church, but not

† In addition to the spiritual manifestations already mentioned as having occurred at this conference of June 3rd-6th, it should be said that, according to John Whitmer's *History of the Church* (ch. v): "The Spirit of the Lord fell upon Joseph in an unusual manner, and he prophesied that John the Revelator was then among the Ten Tribes of Israel who had been led away by Shalmaneser, king of Assyria, to prepare them for their return from their long dispersion, to again possess the land of their fathers. He prophesied many more things that I have not written. After he had prophesied he laid his hands upon Lyman Wight and ordained him to the High Priesthood [i. e., ordained him a High Priest], after the holy order of God. And the Spirit fell upon Lyman, and he prophesied concerning the coming of Christ. He said that there were some in the congregation that should live until the Savior should descend from heaven with a shout, with all the holy angels with Him. He said the coming of the Savior should be like the sun rising in the east, and will cover the whole earth. So with the coming of the Son of Man; yea, He will appear in His brightness and consume all [the wicked] before Him; and the hills will be laid low, and the valleys be exalted, and the crooked be made straight, and the rough smooth. And some of my brethren shall suffer martyrdom for the sake of the religion of Jesus Christ, and seal their testimony of Jesus Christ, and seal their testimony of Jesus with their blood. He saw the heavens opened and the Son of Man sitting on the right hand of the Father, making intercession for his brethren, the Saints. He said that God would work a work in these last days that tongue cannot express and the mind is not capable to conceive. The glory of the Lord shone around.'"

"The congregation at this conference numbered two thousand souls."—Cannon's *Life of Joseph Smith the Prophet*, p. 113.

This was the fourth general conference of the Church, the others were held on the 9th of June, 1830; the 26th of September, 1830; and the 2nd of January, 1831, respectively; and all at Fayette, Seneca County, New York.

and humility, so necessary for the blessing of God to follow prayer, characterized the Saints.

The next day, as a kind continuation of this great work of the last days, I received the following:

*Revelation, given June, 1831.**

1. Behold, thus saith the Lord unto the elders whom he hath called and chosen in these last days, by the voice of his Spirit—

2. Saying: I, the Lord, will make known unto you what I will that ye shall do from this time until the next conference; which shall be held in Missouri, upon the land which I will consecrate unto my people, which are a remant of Jacob, and those who are heirs according to the covenant.

3. Wherefore, verily I say unto you, let my servants Joseph Smith, Jun., and Sidney Rigdon take their journey as soon as preparations can be made to leave their homes, and journey to the land of Missouri.

4. And inasmuch as they are faithful unto me, it shall be made known unto them what they shall do;

5. And it shall also, inasmuch as they are faithful, be made known unto them the land of your inheritance.

6. And inasmuch as they are not faithful, they shall be cut off, even as I will, as seemeth me good.

7. And again, verily I say unto you, let my servant Lyman Wight and my servant John Corrill take their journey speedily;

8. And also my servant John Murdock, and my servant Hyrum Smith, take their journey unto the same place by the way of Detroit.

9. And let them journey from thence preaching the word by the way, saying none other things than that which the prophets and apostles have written, and that which is taught them by the Comforter through the prayer of faith.

10. Let them go two by two, and thus let them preach by the way in every congregation, baptizing by water, and the laying on of the hands by the water's side.

11. For thus saith the Lord, I will cut my work short in righteousness, for the days come that I will send forth judgment unto victory.

12. And let my servant Lyman Wight beware, for Satan desireth to sift him as chaff.

13. And behold, he that is faithful shall be made ruler over many things.

14. And again, I will give unto you a pattern in all things, that ye

* Doctrine and Covenants, sec. lii.

have become high-minded, and have not feared; therefore, but few of them will be gathered with the chosen family. Have not the pride, high-mindedness, and unbelief of the Gentiles, provoked the Holy One of Israel to withdraw His Holy Spirit from them, and send forth His judgments to scourge them for their wickedness? This is certainly the case.

Christ said to His disciples (Mark xvi. ... these signs should follow them tha̱ ... st out devils; they ... p ...

In 1833, Smith prophesied that the wicked of which generation would be swept off the earth? When was this to occur? Who would return after the wicked of his generation were destroyed? To which generation did Smith give his warning? The wicked of Smith's generation were not "swept away" and the ten lost tribes of Israel did not come down from the North Pole during that generation. Smith's prophecy was proven false.

... fall upon the ... glory begins to break forth ... ure of sectarian wickedness, and their iniqu... ... up into view, and the nations of the Gentiles are like the waves of the sea, casting up mire and dirt, or all in commotion, and they are hastily preparing to act the part allotted them, when the Lord rebukes the nations, when He shall rule them with a rod of iron, and break them in pieces like a potter's vessel. The Lord declared to His servants, some eighteen months since, that He was then withdrawing His Spirit from the earth; and we can see that such is the fact, for not only the churches are dwindling away, but there are no conversions, or but very few: and this is not all, the governments of the earth are thrown into confusion and division; and *Destruction*, to the eye of the spiritual beholder, seems to be written by the finger of an invisible hand, in large capitals, upon almost every thing we behold.

And now what remains to be done, under circumstances like these? I will proceed to tell you what the Lord requires of all people, high and low, rich and poor, male and female, ministers and people, professors of religion and non-professors, in order that they may enjoy the Holy Spirit of God to a fulness and escape the judgments of God, which are almost ready to burst upon the nations of the earth. Repent of all your sins, and be baptized in water for the remission of them, in the name of the Father, and of the Son, and of the Holy Ghost, and receive the ordinance of the laying on of the hands of him who is ordained and sealed unto this power, that ye may receive the Holy Spirit of God; and this is according to the Holy Scriptures, and the Book of Mormon; and the only way that man can enter into the celestial kingdom. These are the requirements of the new covenant, or first principles of the Gospel of Christ; then "Add to your faith, virtue; and to virtue, knowledge; and to knowledge, temperance; and to temperance, patience; and to patience, godliness; and to godliness, brotherly kindness; and to brotherly kindness, charity [or love]; for if these things be in you, and abound, they make you that ye shall neither be barren nor unfruitful, in the knowledge of our Lord Jesus Christ."

The Book of Mormon is a record of the forefathers of our western tribes of Indians; having been found through the ministration of an holy angel, and translated into our own language by the gift and power of God, after having been hid up in the earth for the last fourteen hundred years, containing the word of God which was delivered unto them. By it we learn that our western tribes of Indians are descendants from that Joseph which was sold into Egypt, and that the land of America is a promised land unto them, and unto it all the tribes of Israel will come, with as many of the Gentiles as shall comply with the requisitions of the new covenant. But the tribe of Judah will return to old Jerusalem. The city of Zion spoken of by David, in the one hundred and second Psalm, will be built upon the land of America, "And the ransomed of the Lord shall return, and come to Zion with songs and everlasting, joy upon their heads" (Isaiah xxxv: 10); and then they will be delivered from the overflowing scourge that shall pass through the land. But Judah shall obtain deliverance at Jerusalem. See Joel ii:32; Isaiah xxvi: 20 and 21; Jeremiah xxxi: 12; Psalm 1: 5; Ezekiel xxxiv: 11, 12 and 13. These are testimonies that the Good Shepherd will put forth His own sheep, and lead them out from all nations where they have been scattered in a cloudy and dark day, to Zion, and to Jerusalem; besides many more testimonies which might be brought.

And now I am prepared to say by the authority of Jesus Christ, that not many years shall pass away before the United States shall present such a scene of *bloodshed* as has not a parallel in the history of our nation; pestilence, hail, famine, and earthquake will sweep the wicked of this generation from off the face of the land, to open and prepare the way for the return of the lost tribes of Israel from the north country. The people of the Lord, those who have complied with the requirements of the new covenant, have already commenced gathering together to Zion, which is in the state of Missouri; therefore I declare unto you the warning which the Lord has commanded to declare unto this generation, remembering that the eyes of my Maker are upon me, and that to him I am accountable for every word I say, wishing nothing worse to my fellow-men than their eternal salvation; therefore, "Fear God, and give glory to Him, for the hour of His judgment is come." Repent ye, repent ye, and embrace the everlasting

<u>covenant, and flee to Zion, before the overflowing scourge overtake
you, for there are those</u> now living upon the earth whose eyes shall
<u>not be closed in death until they see all these things, which I have
spoken, fulfilled</u>. *Remember* these things; call upon the Lord while He is
near, and seek Him while He may be found, is the exhortation of your
unworthy servant.

[Signed]   JOSEPH SMITH, JUN.

IMPORTANT CORRESPONDENCE WITH THE BRETHREN IN ZION

KIRTLAND, January 14, 1833.

Brother William W. Phelps:

I send you the "olive leaf" which we have plucked from the Tree
of Paradise,* the Lord's message of peace to us; f . . .   h-
ren in Zion indulge in feeling . . .   o
the reonir . . .   f

[Did Smith claim that there would be those of his
own day who would live to see his predictions come
true? Did the people who were alive in 1833 see
with their own eyes the destruction of the wicked
and the coming of the ten lost tribes? To what conclusion about Smith's prophecy does this draw us?]

. . . . Let me say unto
. . . . . .ives, and also all the inhabitants of Zion,
les . . . . . .ord's anger be kindled to fierceness. Repent, repent, is the
voice of God to Zion; and strange as it may appear, yet it is true,
mankind will persist in self-justification until all their iniquity is
exposed, and their character past being redeemed, and that which is
treasured up in their hearts be exposed to the gaze of mankind. I say
to you (and what I say to you I say to all,) hear the warning voice
of God, lest Zion fall, and the Lord sware in His wrath the inhabitants of Zion shall not enter into His rest.

The brethren in Kirtland pray for you unceasingly, for, knowing
the terrors of the Lord, they greatly fear for you. You will see that
the Lord commanded us, in Kirtland, to build a house of God, and
establish a school for the Prophets,† this is the word of the Lord to
us, and we must, yea, the Lord helping us, we will obey; as on con-
ditions of our obedience He has promised us great things; yea, even a
visit from the heavens to honor us with His own presence. We greatly
fear before the Lord lest we should fail of this great honor, which our

*This is the revelation beginning on p. 302, and section lxxxviii of the Doctrine
and Covenants.

†See pp. 310, 311, verses 119-136.

Master proposes to confer on us: we are seeking for humility and great faith lest we be ashamed in His presence. Our hearts are greatly grieved at the spirit which is breathed both in your letter and that of Brother Gilbert's. the very spirit which is wasting the strength of Zion like a pestilence: and if it is not detected and driven from you, it will ripen Zion for the threatened judgments of God. Remember God sees the secret springs of human action. and knows the hearts of all living.

Brother, suffer us to speak plainly. for God has respect to the feelings of His Saints, and He will not suffer them to be tantalized with impunity. Tell Brother Gilbert that low insinuations God hates: but He rejoices in an honest heart, and knows better who is guilty than he does. We send him this warning voice. and let him fear greatly for himself, lest a worse thing overtake him: all we can say by way of conclusion is, if the fountain of our tears be not dried up. we will still weep for Zion. This from your brother who trembles for Zion. and for the wrath of heaven. which awaits her if she repent not.

[Signed]   JOSEPH SMITH, JUN.

P. S.—I am not in the habit of crying peace. when there is no peace: and, knowing the threatened judgments of God. I say. Wo unto them who are at ease in Zion: fearfulness will speedily lay hold of the hypocrite. I did not suspect you had lost the commandments. but thought from your letters you had neglected to read them. otherwise you would not have written as you did.

It is in vain to try to hide a bad spirit from the eyes of them who are spiritual, for it will show itself in speaking and in writing, as well as in all our other conduct. It is also needless to make great pretensions when the heart is not right: the Lord will expose it to the view of His faithful Saints. We wish you to render the *Star* as interesting as possible, by setting forth the rise. progress. and faith of the Church, as well as the doctrine: for if you do not render it more interesting than at present, it will fall. and the Church suffer a great loss thereby.

[Signed]   J. S. JUN.

KIRTLAND MILLS.* GEAUGA CO., OHIO,
January 14, 1833.

From a Conference of Twelve High Priests. to the Bishop. his Council and the Inhabitants of Zion.

Orson Hyde. and Hyrum Smith being appointed by the said confer-

---

* "Kirtland Mills" and "Kirtland" are identical. The name "Kirtland Mills" arose from the existence of some mills on the banks of the branch of the Chagrin river on which Kirtland is situated.

52

322 HISTORY OF THE CHURCH [A. D. 1833]

CHAPTER XXIII.

THE ENJOYMENT OF SPIRITUAL BLESSINGS IN THE CHURCH— THE WORD OF WISDOM.

THIS winter [1832-33] was spent in translating the
Scriptures; in the School of the P ... ts;
and sitting in conf- ... ly

The Enjoy-
ment of
Spiritual
Gifts.

glori-

In 1833, Joseph Smith's father gave a fatherly blessing to his son. What did he prophesy in the name of Christ? Did Smith live until Christ came? What does the passage tell us about the beliefs of Smith and the early Mormons concerning the time of Christ's return?

... ..gaon.

S ... whitney, Hyrum

H ... Joseph Smith, Sen., Samuel

... John Murdock, Lyman E. Johnson,†

Orson Hyde, Ezra Thayer, High Priests; and Levi

Hancock,‡ and William Smith,§ Elders, were assem-

*Zebedee Coltrin was born at Ovid, Seneca county, New York, September 7, 1804. He was the son of John and Sarah Coltrin, and was baptized into the Church soon after its organization.

†Lyman E. Johnson was born in Pomfret, Windsor county, Vermont, October 24, 1811. He was baptized into the Church in February, 1831, by Sidney Rigdon, and was ordained an Elder under the hands of the Prophet Joseph Smith.

‡Levi Ward Hancock was born April 7, 1803, in Old Springfield, Hampden county, Massachusetts. He was the youngest son of Thomas Hancock and Amy Ward Hancock. When Levi was about two years old his family removed from Massachusetts to Ohio, settling in Chagrin, Cayahoga county not far from Kirtland. Here Levi grew to manhood, occupied chiefly in farming with his father. In 1827, however he purchased a farm in Ashtabula county which is in the extreme northeast part of Ohio. He was directly in the pathway of Elders Cowdery, Pratt, Whitmer and Peterson when journeying westward on their mission to the Lamanites; and shortly after they passed through his neighborhood he followed them to Kirtland where he was baptized on the 16th of November 1830, by Elder Parley P. Pratt, and was soon afterwards ordained an Elder under the hands of Oliver Cowdery.

§William Smith was the fifth son of Joseph Smith, Sen., and Lucy Smith. He was born in Royalton, Windsor county, Vermont, March 13, 1811, and was baptized soon after the Church was organized.

bled in conference, on the 22nd day of January, I spoke to the conference in another tongue, and was followed in the same gift by Brother Zebedee Coltrin, and he by Brother William Smith, after which the Lord poured out His Spirit in a miraculous manner, until all the Elders spake in tongues, and several members, both male and female, exercised the same gift. Great and glorious were the divine manifestations of the Holy Spirit. Praises were sung to God and the Lamb; speaking and praying, all in tongues, occupied the conference until a late hour at night, so rejoiced were we at the return of these long absent blessings.

On the 23rd of January, we again assembled in conference; when, after much speaking, singing, *Ordinance of the Washing of Feet.* praying, and praising God, all in tongues, we proceeded to the washing of feet (according to the practice recorded in the 13th chapter of John's Gospel), as commanded of the Lord. Each Elder washed his own feet first, after which I girded myself with a towel and washed the feet of all of them, wiping them with the towel with which I was girded. Among the number, my father presented himself, but before I washed his feet, I asked of him a father's blessing, which he granted by laying his hands upon my head, in the name of Jesus Christ, and <u>declaring that I should continue in the Priest's office until Christ comes</u>. At the close of the scene, Brother Frederick G. Williams, being moved upon by the Holy Ghost, washed my feet in token of his fixed determination to be with me in suffering, or in journeying, in life or in death, and to be continually on my right hand; in which I accepted him in the name of the Lord.

I then said to the Elders, As I have done so do ye; wash ye, therefore, one another's feet; and by *The Elders Pronounced Clean* the power of the Holy Ghost I pronounced them all clean from the blood of this generation: but if any of them should sin wilfully after they were thus cleansed, and sealed up unto eternal life, they should be given over unto the buffetings of

54

affecting prayer, the brethren who went to Zion [in Zion's camp] were requested to take their seats together in a part of the house by themselves.

President Smith then stated that the meeting had been called, because God had commanded it; and it was made known to him by vision* and by the Holy Spirit. He then gave a relation of some of the circumstances attending us while journeying to Zion—our trials, sufferings: and said God had not designed all this for nothing, but He had it in remembrance yet;† and it was the will of God that those who went to Zion, with a determination to lay down their lives, if necessary, should be ordained to the ministry, and go forth to prune the vineyard for the last time, or the coming of the Lord, which was nigh—even fifty-six years should wind up the scene.

The President also said many things; such as the weak things, even the smallest and weakest among us, shall be powerful and mighty and great things shall be accomplished by you from ... shall begin to feel the whi... of God ...

In 1835, what was nigh? How many years yet remained before Christ's return? Fifty-six years added to 1835 pointed to what date for Christ's return? Why would Smith look forward to 1891? Did Christ return in 1891?

t ... ...gation, to know if ..., and they all raised their right hand.

---

* This vision, in which the Prophet evidently saw the order of the Church organization, is several times alluded to by him. By reference to the note on page 181 it will be observed that President Smith there refers to the vision in such a manner as to lead one to believe that he saw that Brigham Young would be one of the Twelve, and Joseph Young President of the Seventies. He also refers to this vision in the revelation which appears in chapter xiv; (Doctrine and Covenants, sec. cvii, 93). Describing the order of the Seventies, he says: "And it is according to the *vision*, showing the order of the Seventy, that there shall be seven Presidents to preside over them, chosen out of the number of the Seventy." It was doubtless in this vision also that the Prophet saw the manner in which the Twelve should be chosen.

† Elder Joseph Young in his "History of the Organization of the Seventies," (page 14) says that the following sentiment was delivered by the Prophet Joseph Smith in an address to the Elders assembled in Kirtland soon after the Seventies were organised: "Brethren, some of you are angry with me, because you did not fight in Missouri; but let me tell you, God did not want you to fight. He could not organize His kingdom with twelve men to open the Gospel door to the nations of the earth, and with seventy men under their direction to follow in their tracks, unless He took them from a body of men who had offered their lives, and who had made as great a sacrifice as did Abraham. Now the Lord has got His Twelve and His Seventy, and there will be other quorums of Seventies called, who will make the sacrifice, and those who have not made their sacrifices and their offerings now, will make them hereafter."

The names of those who went to Zion in the camp are as follows:*

Hazen Aldrich,
Joseph S. Allen,
Isaac Allred,
James Allred,
Martin Allred,
Milo Andrus,
Solomon Angel,
Allen A. Avery,
Almon W. Babbitt
Alexander Badlam,
Samuel Baker,
Nathan Bennett Baldwin,
Elam Barber,
Israel Barlow,
Lorenzo D. Barnes,
Edson Barney,
Royal Barney,
Henry Benner,
Samuel Bent,
Hiram Backman,
Lorenzo Booth,
George W. Brooks,
Albert Brown,
Harry Brown,
Samuel Brown,
John Brownell,
Peter Buchanan,
Alden Burdick,
Harrison Burgess,
David Byur,
William F. Cahoon,
John Carpenter,
John S. Carter,
Daniel Cathcart,
Solon Foster,
Jacob Gates,
Benjamin Gifford,

Alonzo Champlin,
Jacob Chapman,
William Cherry,
John M. Chidester,
Alden Childs,
Nathaniel Childs,
Stephen Childs,
Albert Clements,
Thomas Colborn,
Alanson Colby,
Zera S. Cole,
Zebedee Coltrin,
Libeus T. Coon,
Horace Cowan,
Lyman Curtis,
Mecham Curtis,
Solomon W. Denton,
Peter Doff,
David D. Dort,
John Duncan,
James Dunn,
Philemon Duzette,
Philip Ettleman,
Bradford W. Elliot,
David Elliot,
David Evans,
Asa Field,
Edmund Fisher,
Alfred Fisk,
Hezekiah Fisk,
Elijah Fordham,
George Fordham,
Frederick Forney,
John Fossett,
James Foster,
William S. Ivie,
William Jessop,

* A full list of those who went up to Zion, including women and children, is here published in place of the partial list heretofore published in the History of Joseph Smith in the *Millennial Star*, volume xv, page 205.

56

This excerpt is from the typescript of the *Journal of Oliver Broadman Huntington* (Vol. 2, p. 129).

After Smith prophesied in 1835 that Christ's return would be in fifty-six years, how did those who heard him understand his prophecy? Did Smith ever attempt to correct this belief of his followers? What does this tell us about Smith's opinion of his own prophecies? Did Christ return in either 1890 or 1891?

them count
left, and
redeemed.
Christ is (
natural vi(

hear of
would be
ere looking for
ff even to the

On the 14th of Feb. 1835, Joseph Smith said that God had revealed to him that the coming of Christ would be within 56 years, which being added to 1835 shows that before 1891 and the 14th of Feb. the Savior of the world would make his appearance again upon the earth and the winding up scene take place. In connection with this event, was related by my brother Dimick Huntington, the fact that when Joseph and Hyrum Smith submitted in their feelings to consent to give themselves up to the state mob at Nauvoo Illinois, after they had passed the Mississippi River. Joseph said "if they shed my blood it shall shorten this work 10 years". That taken from 1891 would reduce the time to 1881 which if the true time within which the Savior should come much must be crowded into 6 years.

I went to the April Conference in 1878 and among the many interesting events and rehearsal of events I met with at that conference I heard Dimick tell of an event on the 4th of July 1838 in Far West Missouri after the celebration of the independence of our nation was over, one hour; a small cloud came from the west and passed over the town, and from it was discharged thunderbot which struck the liberty-pole that had been set up on the public square for that occasion, and shivered it into stone.

The fact was immediately communicated to Joseph in whose company Dimick was. He and Dimick immediately walked onto the ground which was literally covered with splinters for quite a distance around where the pole had stood. Jospeh looked at the scene and his face shone white as snow as he said "Thus saith the Lord as this pole has been shivered to stone, so shall this Nation be shivered, and as I walk over these slivers (suiting the movement to the words) so will I walk over the ashes of my enemies." Dimick said Amen.

At another time Joseph was heart to say, in speaking of the redemption of Zion "I will lead this people back to Jackson County."

I testify that every word that Joseph Smith spoke, will be fulfilled that has not been fulfilled.

Another incident Dimick related: "The morning after Joseph reached his family 4 miles east of Quincy Ill. after his escape from the jail and from the hands of the mob in Missouri, he came over to the little log shanty where Dimick and family were stopping, a few rods distant, and said to Dimick "I have had a revelation with regard to you, and God has shown to me that you have got to go among the Lamanites."

After breakfast Dimick presented himself to Joseph with clean shirt on and valice in hand and said he was ready to do. "Go where?" said Joseph. To the Lamanites said D." Joseph smiled and said, "It is not time now but after while your work is with them.

The blessing of Lyman E. Johnson was, in the name of Jesus Christ, that he should bear the tidings of salvation to nations, tongues, and people, until the utmost corners of the earth shall hear the tidings; and that he shall be a witness of the things of God to nations and tongues, and that holy angels shall administer to him occasionally; and that no power of the enemy shall prevent him from going forth and doing the work of the Lord; and that he shall live until the gathering is accomplished, according to the holy prophets; and he shall be like unto Enoch; and his faith shall be like unto his; and he shall be called great among all the living; and Satan shall tremble before him; and he shall see the Savior come and stand upon the earth with power and great glory.

The blessing of Brigham Young was that he should be strong in body, that he might go forth and gather the elect, preparatory to the great day of the coming of the Lord; and that he might be strong and mighty, declaring the tidings to nations that know not God; that h-

talents; that he may ~~~

> If the early Mormons were taught by Smith that Christ would come in their own lifetime around 1890 or 1891, this belief would appear in their expectations. In the blessings recorded, did they believe that these persons would not die before Christ's return but see with their own eyes the coming of the Son of Man? From whom would these men obtain the belief that these men would live until Christ came? It could have come only from their prophet, Joseph Smith.

power to heal the sick, ... give sight to the blind, have power to remove mountains, and all things should be subject to us through the name of Jesus Christ, and angels should minister unto us, and many more things, too numerous to mention." He also adds the following interesting item with reference to the ordinations of that day: "After we [referring to the first three called up to receive ordination] had been thus ordained by these brethren, the First Presidency laid their hands on us and confirmed these blessings and ordinations, and likewise predicted many things which should come to pass." (*Times and Seasons*, vol. vi, p. 868). While these statements make it very clear that the Prophet Joseph did not join with the Three Witnesses in ordaining the Apostles—except in the way of confirming the ordination they received from the Witnesses, as described by Elder Kimball—the minutes of the meeting held February 21st, at which Parley P. Pratt was ordained, state that he was "ordained one of the Twelve by President Joseph Smith, Jun., David Whitmer, and Oliver Cowdery." Martin Harris must have been absent, and the Prophet evidently joined Oliver Cowdery and David Whitmer on that occasion because of the absence of Harris; but whether or not the Prophet was mouth on that occasion does not appear in the minutes or in Elder Pratt's autobiography.

Priesthood is conferred on him, that he may do wonders in the name of Jesus; that he may cast out devils, heal the sick, raise the dead, open the eyes of the blind, go forth from land to land and from sea to sea; and that heathen nations shall even call him God himself, if he do not rebuke them.

Heber C. Kimball's blessing was, in substance, that he shall be made like unto those who have been blessed before him; and be favored with the same blessing. That he might receive visions; the ministration of angels, and hear their voice; and even come into the presence of God; that many millions may be converted by his instrumentality; that angels may waft him from place to place, and that he may stand unto the coming of our Lord, and receive a crown in the Kingdom of our God; that he be made acquainted with the day when Christ shall come; that he shall be made perfect in faith; and that the deaf shall hear, the lame shall walk, the blind shall see, and greater things than these shall he do; that he shall have boldness of speech before the nations, and great power.

A hymn was then sung, "Glorious things of thee are spoken," etc.; and the congreagation was dismissed by President Joseph Smith, Jun.

Sunday, February 15.—The congregation again assembled.

President Cowdery made some observations upon the nature of the meeting, calling upon the Lord for his assistance; after which a number of certificates from brethren that had recently returned from Zion were read and accepted.

President Cowdery then called forward Orson Hyde, David W. Patten and Luke Johnson, and proceeded to their ordinations and blessings.

Orson Hyde's Blessing:—Oliver Cowdery called upon the Lord to smile upon him; that his faith be made perfect, and that the blessings pronounced may be realized; that he be made mighty, and be endued with powers from on high, and go forth to the nations of the earth to proclaim the Gospel, that he may escape all the pollutions of the world; that the angels shall uphold him; and that he shall go forth according to the commandment, both to Jew and Gentile, and to all nations, kingdoms and tongues; that all who hear his voice shall acknowledge him to be a servant of God; that he shall be equal with his brethren in holding the keys of the kingdom; that he may stand on the earth and bring souls till Christ comes. We know that he loves Thee, O, Lord, and may this Thy

60

treated me with the greatest respect.   I showed them the
The Prophet
on "Miller
ism." fallacy of Mr. Miller's *data* concerning the
coming of Christ and the end of the world, or
as it is commonly called, Millerism,* and
preached them quite a sermon; that error was in the
Bible, or the translation of the Bible; that Miller was in
want of correct information upon the subject, and that he
was not so much to blame as the translators. I told
them the prophecies must all be fulfilled; the sun must be
darkened and the moon turned into blood, and many
more things take place before Christ would come.

Monday, 13.—Elder Rigdon came in early in the
morning, and gave a brief history of our second ___ o
Jackson county, Missouri. I th___
and walked ___

When 1843 arrived, what did Smith assert about
Millerism?

___ me that Mr. Rol-
___ get the postoffice, and that Dr. R. D.
___ster was the first to sign the petition. I gave instruc-
tion about a bond for a part of a lot to Brother John Oak-
ley. A quarter before four, went to the printing office
with Brother W. W. Phelps.

I spent the evening at Elder Orson Hyde's. In the
course of conversation I remarked that those brethren
who came here having money, and purchased without the

* Millerism here referred to is the sum of the doctrines taught by William Miller,
an American religious zealot who emphasized in his religious teachings the Millennial Reign of Christ on earth, which reign, he declared, as early as 1831, would
commence in the year 1843. His predictions were based largely upon computations of
time on the prophecies of Daniel and the Book of Revelation. After the great dis-
appointment which came to his followers in 1843, they abandoned all attempts at
fixing the date on which the second advent of Christ would take place, but otherwise continued to believe in the doctrines advocated by Mr. Miller. "There are
several divisions or sects of Adventists, the principal of which are: the Advent
Christians, the largest; the Seventh-day Adventists, much smaller, but more com-
pactly organized; and the Evangelical Adventists, the smallest. The members
of the first two believe in the final annihilation of the wicked, which those of the
third reject. The second observe the seventh day as the Sabbath, and believe in
the existence of the spirit of prophecy among them; they maintain missions in various parts of the world, and a number of institutions at Battle Creek, Michigan,
their headquarters.'—*Century Dictionary*.

Church and without counsel, must be cut off. This, with other observations, aroused the feelings of Brother Dixon, from Salem, Massachusetts, who was present, and he appeared in great wrath.

I received the following communication:

Rigdon's Suggested Petition as to Nauvoo Postmaster.

To the Hon. Mr. Bryant, Second Assistant Postmaster-General:

We, your petitioners, respectfully beg leave to submit that as an attempt is now, by certain individuals, being made to place the post-office in this place into the hands of William H. Rollison, a stranger in our place, and one whose conduct since he came here, has been such as to forbid our having confidence in him; and we do hope and pray, both for ourselves, and that of the public, that he may not receive the appointment of postmaster in Nauvoo, Illinois, but that the present postmaster may continue to hold the office.

Brother Joseph Smith, if the foregoing can have a number of respectable subscribers, I believe Rollinson cannot get the office. I should like to have it so as to send it on Sunday's mail. Respectfully,

SIDNEY RIGDON.

Tuesday, 14.—Sent William Clayton to Quincy, and by him deposited five hundred dollars with General Leach, for Mr. Walsh, for land which lies between my farm and the city, agreeable to my letter to Judge Young.

Read proof of the "Doctrine and Covenants" with Brother Phelps. Read in German from half-past nine to eleven, forenoon. Had the stove removed from the large room in my house into a small brick building which was erected for a smoke house, designing to use it for a mayor's office, until I could build a new one. Had much conversation with Mr. Cowan and various individuals.

Sold Dr. Richards a cow.

Wednesday, 15.—This morning I spent some time in changing the top plate of the office stove, which had been put together wrong. Read a libelous letter in the *Alton Telegraph*, written to Mr. Bassett, of Quincy, concerning Judge Pope, Mr. Butterfield, and the ladies attending my late trial at Springfield; and published the following letter in the *Times and Seasons*:

covenant to preach three-quarters of an hour, otherwise I would give him a good whipping.

Elder Hyde arose and said "Brothers and sisters, I feel as though all had been said that can be said. I can say nothing, but bless you."

At the close of the meeting, Johnson's _____

_____ priests _____ minister in the daily sacrifice.

_____ Huntington returned from Chicago, having had a very cold and severe journey. The ice in Chicago harbor was three feet thick. Brought me a letter from Mr. Justin Butterfield.

Monday, April 3.—Miller's day of judgment has arrived, but it is too pleasant for false prophets.*

At two p. m., started for Carthage, where we arrived about four p. m., and stayed at Jacob B. Backenstos'.

Elders Young and Taylor returned to Nauvoo, having preached four times.

In the evening, reading the Book of Revelation with Elder Hyde and conversing with Esquire Backman.

Upward of $12,000,000 have been recently expended by the French government to fortify the city of Paris.

Tuesday, 4.—Spent five hours preaching to Esquire Backman, Chancery Robinson, and Backenstos. Backman said, "Almost thou persuadest me to be a Christian."

We left Carthage about two p. m., and arrived at Nauvoo, at have-past five.

Wednesday, 5.—Sat with Aldermen Spencer, Wells, Hills, Harris, Whitney and Kimball, associate-justices in the municipal court on a writ of habeas corpus, and discharged Jonathan and Lewis Hoopes from custody.

A branch of the Church organized at Mount Holly, New Jersey, of twenty-five members, by Elder Newton.

* This has reference to William Miller, who predicted that on the 3rd of April, 1843, the Christ would come in glory, and the end of the world would come. See footnote, page 272, this volume.

Thursday, April 6.—I was detained from conference to hear a case of assumpsit, Widow Thompson, *versus* Dixon, until eleven a. m.

The first day of the fourteenth year of the Church of Jesus Christ of Latter-day Saints. Sun shone clear, warm and pleasant. The snow has nearly all disappeared, except a little on the north side of the hill above Zarahemla, Iowa. The ice is about two feet thick on the Mississippi, west of the Temple. A considerable number of the brethren crossed from the Iowa side of the river to the conference, on the ice. The walls of the Temple are from four to twelve feet above the floor.

Minutes of the General Conference. Beginning April 6th, 1843.

An annual conference of the Church of Jesus Christ of Latter-day Saints was convened on the floor of the Temple. There were present—Hyrum Smith, Patriarch; Brigham Young, Heber C. Kimball, Orson Pratt, Wilford Woodruff, John Taylor, George A. Smith, and Willard Richards, of the quorum of the Twelve; Elder Amasa Lyman, and a very large assembly of the elders and Saints.

Elder Brigham Young announced that President Joseph Smith was detained on business, but would be present soon.

Sang a hymn.

Elder Amasa Lyman opened by prayer, and another hymn was sung.

Elder Orson Pratt then read the third chapter of the second epistle of Peter, and spoke upon the subject of the resurrection.

At ten minutes before twelve o'clock, President Joseph Smith and Elders Rigdon and Hyde arrived.

PRESENTATION OF AUTHORITIES.

At twelve o'clock, President Joseph Smith commenced by saying, "We all ought to be thankful for the privilege we enjoy this day of meeting so many of the Saints, and for the warmth and brightness of the heavens over our heads: and it truly makes the countenances of this great multitude to look cheerful and gladdens the hearts of all present." He next stated the object of the meeting, which was—

First. To ascertain the standing of the First Presidency, which he should do by presenting himself before the conference.

Second. To take into consideration the expediency of sending out the

In relation to the half-breed land, it is best described by its name—it is half-breed land; and every wise and judicious person as soon as he can dispose of his effects, if he is not a half ...

wish ...

Smith believed that Christ could not come within what period of time? What would some of the rising generation see before they died? What did Smith prophesy in the name of the Lord God? What date did Smith see as the time of the coming of the Son of man? Did Christ return in 1890 or 1891? What did Smith believe and teach concerning the time of the return of Christ? Did his prophecies fail?

... were preparing, if there was any ... he would talk on other subjects.

THE PROPHET ON THE SECOND COMING OF THE CHRIST.

The question has been asked, can a person not belonging to the Church bring a member before the high council for trial? I answer, No. If I had not actually got into this work and been called of God, I would back out. But I cannot back out: I have no doubt of the truth. Were I going to prophesy, I would say the end [of the world] would not come in 1844, 5, or 6, or in forty years. There are those of the rising generation who shall not taste death till Christ comes.

I was once praying earnestly upon this subject, and a voice said unto me, "My son, if thou livest until thou art eighty-five years of age, thou shalt see the face of the Son of Man." I was left to draw my own conclusions concerning this; and I took the liberty to conclude that if I did live to that time, He would make His appearance. But I do not say whether He will make his appearance or I shall go where He is. I prophesy in the name of the Lord God, and let it be written—the Son of Man will not come in the clouds of heaven till I am eighty-five years old. Then read the 14th chapter of Revelation, 6th and 7th verses—"And I saw another angel fly in the midst of heaven, having the everlasting gospel to preach unto them that dwell on the earth, and to every nation, and kindred, and tongue, and people, saying with a loud voice, Fear God and give glory to Him, for the hour of His judgment is come." And Hosea, 6th chapter, After two days, etc.,—2,520 years; which brings it to 1890. The coming of the Son of Man never will be—never can be till the judgments spoken of for this hour are poured out: which judgments are commenced. Paul says, "Ye are the children of the light, and not of the darkness, that that day should overtake you as a thief in the night." It is not the design of the Almighty to come upon the earth and crush it and grind it to powder, but he will reveal it to His servants the prophets.

Judah must return, Jerusalem must be rebuilt, and the temple, and water come out from under the temple, and the waters of the Dead Sea be healed.   It will take some time to rebuild the walls of the city and the temple, &c : and all this must be done before the Son of Man will make His appearance. There will be wars and rumors of wars, signs in the heavens above and on the earth beneath, the sun turned into darkness and the moon to blood, earthquakes in divers places, the seas heaving beyond their bounds; then will appear one grand sign of the Son of Man in heaven.   But what will the world do? They will say it is a planet, a comet, &c.   But the Son of Man will come as the sign of the coming of the Son of Man, which will be as the light of the morning cometh out of the east.

Choir sang à hymn.

Prayer by W. W. Phelps.

Adjourned at six p. m., until tomorrow morning.

Friday, 7.—

Conference convened at ten a. m.

Singing, prayer by Elder Orson Hyde, and singing.

President Joseph Smith stated that the next business in order was to listen to appeals of elders, &c.; but none appeared.   He was rather hoarse from speaking so long yesterday, and therefore said he would use the boys' lungs today.

The next business in order was to appoint some elders on missions.

Voted that Jedediah M. Grant be sent to preside over the church at Philadelphia.

Voted that Joshua Grant be sent to preside over the church at Cincinnati.

Voted that Pelatiah Brown go to the village of Palmyra, in New York, and raise up a branch of the Church,

Complaints Against the Temple Committee.

The Temple committee was called up for trial.

William Clayton said: Some may expect I am going to be a means of the downfall of the Temple committee.   It is not so: but I design to show that they have been partial.   Elder Higbee has overrun the amount allowed by the trustees about one-fourth.   Pretty much all Elder Higbee's son has received has been in money and store pay.   Higbee's son has had nothing credited on his tithing.   William F. Cahoon has

2. JOSEPH SMITH AND THE TEN LOST TRIBES OF ISRAEL

Joseph Smith prophesied much concerning the ten lost tribes of Israel. Where did Smith say that these tribes lived? When would they make their appearance? Who was prophesying in their midst? Did the early Mormons expect to see the return of the ten lost tribes of Israel in their own generation?

68

*concerning the gathering; and in order to walk by the true light, and
be instructed from on high, on the 3rd of November, 1831, I inquired
of the Lord and received the following important revelation, which has
since been added to the book of Doctrine and Covenants and called the
Appendix. —— A proclamation to the people of the Church to gather
to Zion—This proclamation to be carried by the Elders to the peoples
of the world—Zion and Jerusalem both to be established—The voice
of the Lord to issue from each of these centers—The Lost Tribes to be
remembered by the Lord and to be brought forth from the north
countries—These to receive their blessings at the hand of Ephraim—
Graves of the Saints to be opened at the coming of the Lord—The
doom of those who reject the Lord's message.*

1. Hearken, O ye people of ᵃmy church, saith the Lord your God, and hear ...

out from among the nations ... om ... of

What would the Lord remember? Why were the people of 1831 to prepare? Where did the ten lost tribes supposedly live? What were they to do? Did this happen? Smith predicted in 1831 that the coming of the tribes and Christ was "nigh," but his prediction failed to prove true.

... the voice

... and all the ends of the earth shall see the salvation of their God.

4. Wherefore, prepare ye, prepare ye, O my people; sanctify yourselves; ᶜgather ye together, O ye people of my church, upon the land of Zion, all you that have not been commanded to tarry.

5. Go ye ᶠout from Babylon. Be ye clean that bear the vessels of the Lord.

6. Call your ᵍsolemn assemblies, and speak often one to another. And let every man call upon the name of the Lord.

7. Yea, verily I say unto you again, the time has come when the voice of the Lord is unto you: ʰGo ye out of Babylon; ⁱgather ye

... the Lord unto all people: "Go ye forth unto the land of Zion, that the borders of my people may be enlarged, and that her ᵏstakes may be strengthened, and that Zion may go forth unto the regions round about.

10. Yea, let the cry go forth among all people: Awake and arise and go forth to ᵐmeet the Bridegroom; behold and lo, the Bridegroom cometh; go ye out to meet him. Prepare yourselves for the ⁿgreat day of the Lord.

11. Watch, therefore, for ye know neither the day nor the hour.

12. Let them, therefore, who are ᵒamong the Gentiles flee unto Zion.

13. And let them who be of ᵖJudah flee unto Jerusalem, unto

a, see a, sec. 1.   b, see d, sec. 36.   c, see e, sec. 1.   d, Isa. 52:10.   e, see
j, sec. 10.   f, see j, sec. 10.   g, see 2r, sec. 88.   h, see j, sec. 10.   i, see j, sec.
10.   j, see a, sec. 1.   k, see b, sec. 1.   l, see o, sec. 18.   m, see o, sec. 18.
n, see j, sec. 10.   o, see g, sec. 87; and a, sec. 82.   p, see e, sec. 1.   q, see e,
sec. 1.   r, see j, sec. 10.   s, see o, sec. 45.

the mountains of the Lord's house.

14. Go ye out from among the nations, 'even from Babylon, from the midst of wickedness, which is spiritual Babylon.

15. But verily, thus saith the Lord, let not your flight be in "haste, but let all things be prepared before you; and he that goeth, let him not 'look back lest sudden destruction shall come upon him.

16. Hearken and hear, O ye inhabitants of the earth. Listen, ye elders of "my church together, and hear the voice of the Lord; for he calleth upon all men, and he commandeth 'all men everywhere to repent.

17. For behold, the Lord God hath ʸsent forth the angel crying through the midst of heaven, saying: Prepare ye the way of the Lord, and make his paths straight, for the ᶻhour of his coming is nigh—

18. When the Lamb shall ²ᵃstand upon Mount Zion, and with him a hundred and forty-four thousand, having his Father's name written on their foreheads.

19. Wherefore, prepare ye for the ²ᵇcoming of the Bridegroom; go ye, go ye out to meet him.

20. For behold, he shall ²ᶜstand upon the mount of Olivet, and upon the mighty ocean, even the great deep, and upon the islands of the sea, and ²ᵈupon the land of Zion.

21. And he shall ²ᵉutter his voice out of Zion, and he shall ²ᶠspeak from Jerusalem, and his ²ᵍvoice shall be heard among all people;

22. And it shall be a voice as the ²ʰvoice of many waters, and as the voice of a great thunder, which ²ⁱshall break down the mountains, and the ²ʲvalleys shall not be found.

23. He shall command the great deep, and it shall be driven back into the north countries, and the ²ᵏislands shall become one land;

24. And the land of Jerusalem and the land of Zion shall be turned back into their own place, and the earth shall be like as it was in the days ²ˡbefore it was divided.

25. And the Lord, even the Savior, shall stand in the midst of his people, and shall ²ᵐreign over all flesh.

26. And they who are in the ²ⁿnorth countries shall come in remembrance before the Lord; and their prophets shall hear his voice, and shall no longer stay themselves; and they shall smite the rocks, and the ice shall flow down at their presence.

27. And an ²ᵒhighway shall be cast up in the midst of the great deep.

28. Their enemies shall become a prey unto them,

29. And in the ²ᵖbarren deserts there shall come forth pools of living water; and the ²ᵠparched ground shall no longer be a thirsty land.

30. And they shall bring forth their rich treasures unto the children of Ephraim, my servants.

31. And the boundaries of the ²ʳeverlasting hills shall tremble at their presence.

32. And there shall they fall down and be crowned with glory,

---

t, see j, sec. 10.   u, see j, sec. 10.   v, Gen. 19:26.   w, see a, sec. 1.
x, see b, sec. 1.   y, see secs. 13, 27.   z, see e, sec. 1.   2a, Rev. 14:1.   2b, see
e, sec. 1.   2c, 45:48.   2d, 3 Ne. 20:22.   21:25.   2e, Joel 3:16.   2f, Joel 3:16.
2g, 45:49.   2h, 110:3.   Rev. 19:6.   2i, ver. 40.   49:23.   Isa. 40:4.   2j, see 2i.
2k, ver. 24.   Rev. 6:15.   2l, Gen. 10:25.   Isa. 62:4.   2m, see e, sec. 1.   2n,
110:11.   2o, Isa. 51:9—11.   35:8—10.   2p, Isa. 35:6, 7.   2q, Isa. 35:6, 7.
2r, Hab. 3:60.

70

taking to carry on this work of their own accord, the time will come when God will cause the stone of the mountains to roll, and then it will roll down and build up the central city of Zion, and that, too, long before this gathering from the distant nations shall cease. I do not know how much before the ten tribes will come from the north; but after Zion is built in Jackson County, and after the Temple is built upon that spot of ground where the corner stone was laid in 1831; after the glory of God in the form of a cloud by day shall rest upon that Temple, and by night the shining of a flaming fire will fill the whole heavens round about; after every dwelling place upon Mount Zion shall be clothed upon as with a pillar of fire by night, and a cloud by day, about that period of time, the ten tribes will be heard of, away in the north, a great company, as Jeremiah says, coming down from the northern regions, coming to sing in the height of the latter-day Zion. Their souls will be as a watered garden, and they will not sorrow any more at all, as they have been doing during the twenty-five hundred long years they have dwelt in the Arctic regions. They will come, and the Lord will be before their ___ will utter h___

shall be crowned with glory under the hands of the servants of God living in those days, the children of Ephraim, crowned with certain blessings that pertain to the Priesthood, that they could not receive in their own lands. In that day will be set apart twelve thousand out of each of these ten tribes—one hundred and twenty thousand persons ordained to the High Priesthood, after the order of the Son of God, to go forth to all people, nations, kindreds and tongues, for the salvation of the remnants of Israel in the four quarters of the earth, to bring as many as will come unto the Church of the firstborn. Thus God will have twelve thousand out of all the tribes of Israel to fulfill his purposes; and when they have completed his work here on the earth, they will be called home to Zion, be crowned with glory and stand upon Mount Zion and sing the song of the redeemed, the song of the hundred and forty-four thousand, and the Father's name will be written in their foreheads.

By and by, when all things are prepared—when the Jews have received their scourging, and Jesus has descended upon the Mount of Olives, the ten tribes ___

When would the ten tribes show up? From what region will they come? How long have they lived in the Arctic regions? When was the cornerstone laid for the temple? Is there any scientific or archeological evidence to indicate that the ten lost tribes of Israel were living in the Arctic and had been there for twenty-five hundred years? The only rational conclusion one can make concerning this prophecy is that it is false.

___ the joy ___ whole earth. " Beautiful for
they come to the height of Zion they ___ situation is Mount Zion on the sides of the north, the city of the great King."

hear my voice"—that is, he would minister to them, and they would see Him and they would hear His voice. And the instruction that he gave, they were ~~~ write ~~~

~~~ contained in the Jewish record, but the knowledge of God contained in all the records. The Book of Mormon informs us that the ten tribes in the north country will have a record as well as the Jews, a Bible of their own, if you please. Indeed Jesus after having instructed the remnant of Joseph upon this land and revealed to them His gospel, said to them, " But now I go unto the Father, and also to show myself unto the lost tribes of Israel, for they are not lost unto the Father, for He knoweth whither He hath taken them." And it was predicted concerning them by one of the ancient American prophets, who lived in those days, that when God should bring these ten tribes from the north country, they would bring their records with them. And it should come to pass that they should have the records of the Nephites, and the Nephites should have the records of the Jews, and the Jews and the Nephites should have the records of the lost tribes of the house of Israel, and the lost tribes of Israel should have the records of the Nephites and the Jews. " It shall come to pass that I will gather my people together, and I will also gather my word in one." Not only the people are to be gathered from the distant portions of our globe, but their records, or bibles, will also be united in one.

In the good old book believed in by the world of Christianity, we have a prophecy which may b~ ~ in the 37th ~~~

~~~ write upon it, For ~~~, and for the children of Israel, his companions; then take another stick, and write upon it, For Joseph, the stick of Ephraim, and for all the house of Israel his companions.

"And join them one to another into one stick, and they shall become one in thine hand.

"And when the children of thy people shall speak unto thee, saying, Wilt thou not show us what thou meanest by these?

"Say unto them, Thus saith the Lord God; Behold, I will take the stick of Joseph, which is in the hand of Ephraim, and the tribes of Israel his fellows, and will put them with him, even with the stick of Judah, and make them one stick, and they shall be one in mine hand.

"And the sticks wherein thou writest shall be in thine hand before thine eyes."

Why was he commanded to do this simple thing, for surely it would be considered simple in our day for a man to take two sticks, writing upon one for Judah, and upon another one for Joseph, and then joining the two sticks together, and holding them up in his hands to become one? If we were to undertake to preach in this way the people would think we were insane. But it was a familiar way by which the Lord intended to instruct his people, and the interpretation is this: These two sticks were to represent what the Lord would do. Says he, " When the children of thy people shall speak unto thee saying, Wilt thou not show us what thou

thority of the Melchizedek Priesthood was manifested and conferred for the first time upon several of the Elders.* It was clearly evident that the Lord gave us power in proportion to the work to be don~ ~nd strength according to the race set befor~ ~ce and help as our needs required ~ ~e-vailed; several were o~~

According to Smith, who was alive and prophesying among the ten lost tribes of Israel? How old is the Apostle John if he is still alive? If John died as history records, what conclusion must be arrived at concerning Joseph Smith's claim to be an inspired prophet?

* A mis~~

"T~~

~~nize-
p~ ~uie.) The Prophet does
nc ~ ~.en for the first time in the Church
It ~ ~~ the special office of High Priest was for
the ~ ~men in this dispensation, except in so far as Apostles
are ~ ~ (Doctrine and Covenants, sec. lxxxiv: 63); and of course as
there ~men who had been ordained to the apostleship before this conference of
June, 1831, in that manner there had been High Priests in the Church, but not
otherwise.

† In addition to the spiritual manifestations already mentioned as having occurred at this conference of June 3rd-6th, it should be said that, according to John Whitmer's *History of the Church* (ch. v): "The Spirit of the Lord fell upon Joseph in an unusual manner, and he prophesied that John the Revelator was then among the Ten Tribes of Israel who had been led away by Shalmaneser, king of Assyria, to prepare them for their return from their long dispersion, to again possess the land of their fathers. He prophesied many more things that I have not written. After he had prophesied he laid his hands upon Lyman Wight and ordained him to the High Priesthood [i. e., ordained him a High Priest], after the holy order of God. And the Spirit fell upon Lyman, and he prophesied concerning the coming of Christ. He said that there were some in the congregation that should live until the Savior should descend from heaven with a shout, with all the holy angels with Him. He said the coming of the Savior should be like the sun rising in the east, and will cover the whole earth. So with the coming of the Son of Man; yea, He will appear in His brightness and consume all [the wicked] before Him; and the hills will be laid low, and the valleys be exalted, and the crooked be made straight, and the rough smooth. And some of my brethren shall suffer martyrdom for the sake of the religion of Jesus Christ, and seal their testimony of Jesus Christ, and seal their testimony of Jesus with their blood. He saw the heavens opened and the Son of Man sitting on the right hand of the Father, making intercession for his brethren, the Saints. He said that God would work a work in these last days that tongue cannot express and the mind is not capable to conceive. The glory of the Lord shone around.'"

"The congregation at this conference numbered two thousand souls."—Cannon's *Life of Joseph Smith the Prophet*, p. 113.

This was the fourth general conference of the Church, the others were held on the 9th of June, 1830; the 26th of September, 1830; and the 2nd of January, 1831, respectively; and all at Fayette, Seneca County, New York.

and humility, so necessary for the blessing of God to follow prayer, characterized the Saints.

The next day, as a kind continuation of this great work of the last days, I received the following:

Revelation, given June, 1831.*

1. Behold, thus saith the Lord unto the elders whom he hath called and chosen in these last days, by the voice of his Spirit—

2. Saying: I, the Lord, will make known unto you what I will that ye shall do from this time until the next conference, which shall be held in Missouri, upon the land which I will consecrate unto my people, which are a remant of Jacob, and those who are heirs according to the covenant.

3. Wherefore, verily I say unto you, let my servants Joseph Smith, Jun., and Sidney Rigdon take their journey as soon as preparations can be made to leave their homes, and journey to the land of Missouri.

4. And inasmuch as they are faithful unto me, it shall be made known unto them what they shall do;

5. And it shall also, inasmuch as they are faithful, be made known unto them the land of your inheritance.

6. And inasmuch as they are not faithful, they shall be cut off, even as I will, as seemeth me good.

7. And again, verily I say unto you, let my servant Lyman Wight and my servant John Corrill take their journey speedily;

8. And also my servant John Murdock, and my servant Hyrum Smith, take their journey unto the same place by the way of Detroit.

9. And let them journey from thence preaching the word by the way, saying none other things than that which the prophets and apostles have written, and that which is taught them by the Comforter through the prayer of faith.

10. Let them go two by two, and thus let them preach by the way in every congregation, baptizing by water, and the laying on of the hands by the water's side.

11. For thus saith the Lord, I will cut my work short in righteousness, for the days come that I will send forth judgment unto victory.

12. And let my servant Lyman Wight beware, for Satan desireth to sift him as chaff.

13. And behold, he that is faithful shall be made ruler over many things.

14. And again, I will give unto you a pattern in all things, that ye

* Doctrine and Covenants, sec. lii.

3. JOSEPH SMITH AND MEN ON THE MOON

Do men and women inhabit the moon? Are there inhabitants on the sun as well? What do these moon people look like? How long do they live? Why did the early Mormons believe that the sun and the moon were inhabited? Who taught this doctrine? If Smith was the one who taught them this and the teaching was carried on by Brigham Young and other Mormon prophets, what does this mean? If there are no people living on the moon or on the sun, does this mean that Joseph Smith, Brigham Young, etc., were false prophets? Only the historic Mormon documents can answer these questions.

From "George Laub's Nauvoo Journal," *BYU Studies*, Vol. 18, No. 2, Winter 1978

judges among the gods So John ch 10th, 31 & 33 verse Jesus ansred them, Is it not writen in your law, I say ye are gods. 35, if ye call them gods unto whome the word of [God] came & the Scripture cannot be broken. See Revelations 1 Chapter, 6 Vers And hass made us kings and Priests unto & hiss father, to him be glory & dominion for ever. this showing us of more gods then one. but as we are only to worship the one we must know how to pay reverence to him & where his abode is & what relation we sustain to him and how to aproach him & unless he reveals himself to us . . . . . con-cerning him. Therefore by . . . . .

God . . . . .

> **As early as 1843, what did Hyrum Smith (Joseph's brother) teach? Did Smith contradict or correct the moon-people and sun-people doctrine?**

. . . . . come to pass that in . . . . . presence or Redemption for your dead & in Jeru . . . . . and those that (will) not be redeemed or do not be redeemed. the Antions [Ancients] Shall come & redeem them in their glory. Then Saviours, or in other words gods, will come on mount Zion etc.

By Joseph Smith April 20 1843

The Scripture say I and my father are one & again that the Father, Son, & Holy Ghost are one, 1 John 5 ch., 7 vers. But these three agree in the same thing & did the Saviour pray to the Father, I pray not for the world but those [w]home he gave me out of the world that we might be one, or to Say be of one mind in the unity of the faith.

But Every one being a diffrent or Seperate persons & so is God, & Jesus Christ & the Holy Ghost. Seperate persons. But they all agree in one or the self same thing But the Holy Ghost is yet a Spiritual body and waiting to take to himself a body, as the Savior did or as God did or the gods before them took bodies. For the Saviour says the work that my Father did do I also & those are the works. He took himself as a body & then laid down his life that he might take it up again & the Scripture say those who will obey the commandments shall be heirs of God & Joint heirs with Jesus Christ. We then also took bodys to lay them down, to take them up again, & the Sperit itself bears witness with our spirits that we are the children of God & if children then heirs and Joint heirs with Jesus Christ if so be that we suffer with him in the flesh that we may be also glorified to gether. See Romans 8 ch., 16 & 17 Vers

Bro Hurum Smith April 27th 1843

Concerning the *plurality of gods & worlds.*

Now I say unto you that there are lords meny & gods meny. But to us there is but one God the Father & Jesus Christ the first begotten, who is made Equil with God so that he himself is a god. And now the work that the Father done did he don also & So there is a whole trane & lemage of gods, & this world was created by faith & works. The same as if a man would build a house. He knows where the materials are & believs he could do the work of

Neither this sermon nor any reference to it appears in the *History of The Church.*

that building, for he understood the Scence of building & by faith he gained the work with his own hands and compleated that Building. The Same way was this world by faith & works & by understanding the principle. It was made by the hands of God or gods. It was made of Element or in other words of cavus [chaos]. It was in cayatick form from all Eternity and will be to all Eternity. & again they held counsil together that they might ro[l]l this world into form as all others are made, Showing you by the building of a house as a sample or as figure in my Father's house are many mantions, or in my Father's world are meny worlds. I will goe & prepar a place for you, & then it there are meny worlds then there must be meny gods, for every Star that we see is a world and is inhabited the same as this world is peopled. The Sun & Moon is inhabited & the Stars & (Jesus Christ is the light of the Sun, etc.). The Stars are inhabited the same as this Earth But eny of them are larger then this Earth, & meny that we cannot see without a telliscope are larger then this Earth. They are under the same order as this Earth is undergoing & undergoing the same change. There was & is a first man Adam and also a Saviour in the Meredien of times, the same computing times and all things in order. Meny things are to be considered that will bring knowledg to our understanding, but the foolish understand not these things for this world was paternd after the former world or after Mansions above.

By Heber C. Kimble[*]

If we become to be kings & priests unto God we must make our children just as hapy as they can be & we must be rulers over them, to give them their inheritences. And all these Seventies must & will become presidants before Ten years from this 31st day of December 1844, for this work will rool on yet for Two Thousand years. There was much spoken concerning the times in Missouri & the time will come that we must goe forth to put our Enemys to flight by the power of the holy ghost. But the time hass not yet come for us to run through the city before it is clensed, for it is not yet time & Preserve our President & his wife for we must receave our endewments through them. But it must be done in order, every one in & at his time as it comes through the chanel comencing at the head, & be patient & wait till your time & turn comes.

By President Brigham Young[*]

Commencing the Kingdom. At the dedication of the Seventys Hall. Now concerning the organisation of the kingdom of God is brought to pass. The Sav-

---

[*] These remarks seem to have been given at the dedication of the Seventies' Hall in late December, 1844 The official minutes briefly report two speeches by Heber C. Kimball on 26 and 27 December, both of which were apparently somewhat similar to this in subject matter, but neither of which is clearly the one Laub's report is based on (*HC*, 7:335 and 339–40).

[*] The dedication of the Seventies' Hall continued from Thursday, 26 December 1844, through Monday, 30 December There were many lengthy and impressive speeches, new hymns presented by W. W Phelps and John Taylor, and two dedicatory prayers, the first by Brigham Young John D Lee kept the minutes, which first appeared in the *Times and Seasons* (6:794–99) and then were expanded for the *History of The Church* (7:330–45) But Lee gave no indication of any speech by Brigham Young, though he does provide a summary of a similar speech on a similar subject by Orson Pratt. In the copy of this journal included in the first of his three-volume set, Laub added a summary of a speech Amasa Lyman apparently gave on 29 December (which is not similar to Lee's re-

bad for your growing, impressionable girls. Comedies, farces, operas of the lighter sorts, dramas, concerts and negro shows are good to cheer and amuse all, even the dear innocent girls, so once a week, say, we will allow Our Girl to visit a theatre. Out of door sports in ...

their pleasure. Don't scowl and be cross when the young visitors come in, but welcome them with a smile, and do you take the lead of their fun and frolic; at least tak... strings in ...

[overlay box:] What did this Mormon magazine in 1892 state concerning Smith's prophecy about people on the moon? How long did these moon people live and how tall were they? Where did the ten lost tribes of Israel live? What is the shape of the earth according to Smith? Are there moon people? Has anyone ever found a warm fruitful country at the North Pole? Is the planet earth shaped like a lemon? What is the only logical conclusion we can draw concerning this prophecy?

... consider it an honor to be invited there. In one last word let me call your attention to the fact that you must insist upon one especial point in every sort and kind of amusement and that last word, that especial point, is *moderation.*

... that is at all possi... you are kept at home, you will find your girls will be willing to get most of their innocent "fun" at home, if you will allow them to invite their young friends to share

---

OUR SUNDAY CHAPTER.

THE INHABITANTS OF THE MOON.
O. B. HUNTINGTON.

ASTRONOMERS and philosophers have, from time almost immemorial until very recently, asserted that the moon was uninhabited, that it had no atmosphere, etc. But recent discoveries, through the means of powerful telescopes, have given scientists a doubt or two upon the old theory.

Nearly all the great discoveries of men in the last half century have, in one way or another, either directly or indirectly, contributed to prove Joseph Smith to be a Prophet.

As far back as 1837, I know that he said the moon was inhabited by men and women the same as this earth, and that they lived to a greater age than we do—that they live generally to near the age of a.1000 years.

He described the men as averaging near six feet in height, and dressing quite uniformly in something near the Quaker style.

In my Patriarchal blessing, given by the father of Joseph the Prophet, in Kirtland, 1837, I was told that I should preach the gospel before I was 21 years of age; that I should preach the gospel to the inhabitants upon the islands of the sea, and—to the inhabitants of the moon, even the planet you can now behold with your eyes.

The first two promises have been fulfilled, and the latter may be verified.

From the verification of two promises we may reasonably expect the third to be fulfilled also.

———

ONE truth after another men are finding out by the wisdom and inspiration given of God to them.

The inspiration of God caused men to hunt for a new continent until Columbus discovered it. Men have lost millions of dollars, and hundreds of lives to find a country beyond the north pole; and they will yet find that country—a warm, fruitful country, inhabited by the ten tribes of Israel, a country divided by a river, on one side of which lives the half tribe of Manasseh, which is more numerous than all the others. So said the Prophet. At the same time he described the shape of the earth at the poles as being a rounded elongation, and drew a diagram of it in this form:

which any one can readily see will allow the sun's rays to fall so near perpendicular to the center that that part of the earth may be warmed and made fruitful. He quoted scripture in proof of his theory which says that "the earth flieth upon its wings in the midst of the creations of God," and said that there was a semblance in the form of the earth that gave rise to the saying.

CEDAR FORT, Utah,
Feb. 6, 1892.

———•———

HOUSEHOLD DEPARTMENT.

DAINTY HOUSEKEEPING.

LUCY PAGE STELLE.

I HAVE in mind, as I write, one of those mirth-provoking cartoons that give one some suggestion of truth as well. It was two pictures of a kitchen that was prepared for the new servant. The first showed how tastily it was fixed with a flowering plant in the window, a pretty chintz ruffle on the mantle shelf with a few tasteful ornaments, with a comfortable rocking chair with a neat tidy upon it, and so on. The next picture showed the kitchen after Bridget had *unfixed* the place to suit herself. The flowering plant was reduced to a few dry stems. Some utensils were on the shelf, the tidy from the rocking chair was gone, and perfect havoc was wrought generally by the iconoclastic Bridget. To be sure, Bridget's early education was not conducive to elegance and refinement of surroundings, her only thought being the accomplishment of what she is paid to do.

It seems to me that a lady's sur-

From *The Journal of Oliver Broadman Huntington*

"Inhabitants of the Moon
are more of a uniform size than
the inhabitants of the Earth,
being about 6 feet in height.
The...

According to this early Mormon diary, from whom
did this Mormon learn about people on the moon?

...style, or
the one fashion of dress,

They live to be very
old; comeing generally, near
a thousand years."

This is the description of
them as given by Joseph
the Seer, and he could
"See" whatever he asked the
Father in the name of Jesus
to see.

I heard him say that
"he could ask what he
would of the Father, in the
name of Jesus and it
would be granted and
I have no more doubt of it
than I have that the Mob
killed him.

Joseph Smith the Prophet
said to some boys that were
in swimming in the river
at Nauvoo, "come out of the
water boys & stay out, for I
do not want to be obliged to
take time to follow you to
the graveyard".

That crowd of little boys
were in the habit of almost
daily congregating on the
bank of the Mississippi river
for a long bathe in the
warm water in Mid Summ-
er. Joseph had seen them
often & was inspire to make
the above remark.

The boys paid no attention
to the warning & in a week
or more he did follow some
of them into the graveyard.

From *Journal of Discourses*, Vol. XIII

" fanatic " is not applied to professors of religion only. How was it with Dr. Morse, when shut up in the attic of an old building in Baltimore for more than a year, with a little wire stretched round the room, experimenting upon it with his battery, he told a friend that by means of that he could sit there and talk to Congress in Washington? Was he not considered a fanatic, and wild, and crazy? Certainly he was; and so it was with Robert Fulton, when he was conducting his experiments with steam and endeavoring to apply it so as to propel a vessel through the water. And all great disc——

inhabitants of that sphere you find that the most learned are as ignorant in regard to them as the most ignorant of their fellows. So it is with regard to the inhabitants of the sun. Do you think it is inhabited? I rather think it is. Do you think there is any life there? No question of it; it was not made in vain. It was made to give light to those who dwell upon it, and to other planets; and so will this earth when it is celestialized. Every planet in its first rude, organic state receives not the glory of God upon it, but is opaque; but when ——

Since Smith taught the moon-people doctrine, it would be carried on by his immediate successors such as Brigham Young. What did Young teach? Did he claim to be a prophet like Smith? If the sun and the moon are *not* inhabited, what conclusion can we draw about Smith's and Young's prophetic claims?

...ideas as facts, and try to establish a superstructure upon a false foundation. They are the fanatics; and however ardent and zealous they may be, they may reason or argue on false premises till doomsday, and the result will be false. If our religion is of this character we want to know it; we would like to find a philosopher who can prove it to us. We are called ignorant; so we are: but what of it? Are not all ignorant? I rather think so. Who can tell us of the inhabitants of this little planet that shines of an evening, called the moon? When we view its face we may see what is termed " the man in the moon," and what some philosophers declare are the shadows of mountains. But these sayings are very vague, and amount to nothing; and when you inquire about the

...ite from black, brown from gray, and so on? Did you acquire this faculty by your own power? Did any of you impart this power to me or I to you? Not at all. Then where did we get it from? From a superior Being. When I think of these few little things with regard to the organization of the earth and the people of the earth, how curious and how singular it is! And yet how harmonious and beautiful are Nature's laws! And the work of God goes forward, and who can hinder it, or who can stay His hand now that He has commenced His kingdom?

This brings us right back to this Gospel. God has commenced His kingdom on the earth. How intricate it is, and how difficult for a man to understand if he be not enlightened by the Spirit of God! How can we understand it? O, we have nothing

4. JOSEPH SMITH AND THE TEMPLE LOT

In Independence, Missouri, there is an empty lot that bears a historical plaque which identifies the lot as the exact spot where Joseph Smith said a Mormon temple would be built in his own generation. The original cornermarkers have been found and are on public display. What exactly did Smith say about this temple? When would it be built? Would any other place be acceptable? If no temple was built in Smith's generation, what would this mean about Smith's claim to be a true prophet of God? How did the early Mormons interpret Smith's prophecy that a temple would be built on that spot "in that generation"? Did they interpret it as referring to the generation of those living in 1832? As the years passed, did the Mormon leaders feel any pressure to build a temple on this spot while someone was still alive from the 1832 generation? How many years have passed since 1832? If there is no temple on the temple lot and the 1832 generation has passed away, what logical implication must be drawn? The historic documents will show us.

according to the laws of the land.

4. All children have [b]claim upon their parents for their maintenance until they are of age.

5. And after that, they have [c]claim upon the church, or in other words upon the Lord's storehouse, if their parents have not wherewith to give them inheritances.

6. And the storehouse shall be kept by the [d]consecrations of the church; and widows and orphans shall be provided for, as also the poor. Amen.

SECTION 84.

REVELATION *given through Joseph Smith the Prophet, at Kirtland, Ohio, September 22 and 23, 1832. During the month of September, Elders had begun to return from their missions in the eastern States, and to make reports of their labors. It was while they were together in this season of joy that the following communication was received. The Prophet designates it a Revelation on Priesthood. See History of the Church, vol. 1, p. 286. —— A Temple to be built in the land of Zion during this generation—The line of the Holy Priesthood from Moses back to Adam—Relation between the Holy Priesthood and the Lesser Priesthood—Bearers of these two Priesthoods called the sons of Moses and of Aaron respectively—Blessings and privileges of those who attain to these Priesthoods—The bondage of sin—The new and everlasting covenant—Gifts of the spirit specified—The Lord calls his servants, friends—Missionary service imperative—Plagues impending because of wickedness.*

1. A revelation of Jesus Christ unto his servant Joseph Smith, Jun., and six elders, as they united their hearts and lifted their voices on high.

2. Yea, the word of the Lord concerning his church, established in the last days for the restoration of his people, as he has spoken by the mouth of his prophets, and for the [a]gathering of his saints to stand upon Mount Zion, which shall be the city of [b]New Jerusalem.

3. Which city shall be built, [c]beginning at the temple lot, which is appointed by the finger of the Lord, in the western boundaries of the State of Missouri, and dedicated by the hand of Joseph Smith, Jun., and others with whom the Lord was well pleased.

4. Verily this is the word of the Lord, that the city New Jerusalem shall be built by the gathering of the saints, [d]beginning at this place, even the place of the temple, which temple shall be [e]reared in this generation.

5. For verily this generation shall not [f]all pass away until an house shall be built unto the Lord, and a [g]cloud shall rest upon it, which cloud shall be even the glory of the Lord, which shall fill the house.

---

b, 68:25—31.   c. see a, sec. 51.   d, see n, sec. 42.   SEC. 84:   a, see j, sec. 10.   b, see d. sec. 28.   c, see c, sec. 57.   d, see c, sec. 57.   e, 124:49—54. f, ver. 31.   45:31.   112:33.   g, vers. 31, 32.   Ex. 13:21.   16:10.   19:9, 40:34. Lev. 16:2.   1 Kings 8:10.

raised up, being filled with the Holy Ghost from his mother's womb.

28. For he was bap~~ ... he was ~~ ...

~~are sanctified by the Spirit unto the *renewing~~ ...

In 1832, what did Smith prophesy would be built? Within what generation would this city and its temple be built? Would some of the people who were alive in 1832 see the city and temple built before they died? How many years have passed since 1832? Is there a Mormon city and temple in Jackson County, Missouri? The city and temple were never built and the 1832 generation has passed away. At what conclusion must we arrive concerning Smith's prophecy?

teac ... necessary *ap ... ...ges belonging to the lesser priesthood, which priesthood was confirmed upon Aaron and his sons.

31. Therefore, as I said *concerning the sons of Moses—for the sons of Moses and also the sons of Aaron shall offer an acceptable offering and sacrifice in the house of the Lord, which house shall be built unto the Lord in *this generation, upon the *consecrated spot as I have appointed—

32. And the sons of Moses and of Aaron shall be *filled with the glory of the Lord, upon Mount Zion in the Lord's house, whose sons are ye; and also many whom I have called and sent forth to build up my church.

33. For whoso is faithful unto the obtaining these two priesthoods of which I have spoken, and the magnifying their calling,

39. And this is according to the oath and covenant which belongeth to the priesthood.

40. Therefore, all those who receive the priesthood, receive this *oath and covenant of my Father, which he cannot break, neither can it be moved.

41. But whoso breaketh this covenant after he hath received it, and altogether turneth therefrom, shall *not have forgiveness of sins in this world nor in the world to come.

42. And wo unto all those who come not unto this *priesthood which ye have received, which I now confirm upon you who are present this day, by mine own voice out of the heavens; and even I have given the *heavenly hosts and mine angels charge concerning you.

43. And I now give unto you a commandment to beware concerning yourselves, to give dili-

2b, Matt. 3:3.   2c, 93:17.   Matt. 28:18.   John 3:35.   5:22.   13:3.   17:2.   Rom.
14:9.   1 Cor. 15:27.   Phil. 2:9—11.   Heb. 1:2.   1 Pet. 3:22.   Rev. 17:14.   2d,
107:7, 11, 22—26, 36, 37.   2e, see i, sec. 68.   2f, 107:85—88.   2g, vers. 6, 32.
2h, see f.   2i, ver. 3.   See c, sec. 57.   2j, see g.   2k, 89:18—21.   Gal. 3:27—
29.   2l, see x, sec. 35.   2m, ver. 99.   See j, sec. 10.   2n, vers. 88—90.   112:20.
2o, John 13:20.   2p, see x, sec. 35.   2q, see d, sec. 50.   2r, vers. 41, 48.
2s, 41:1.   76:29—37.   2t, see i, sec. 68.   2u, ver. 88.   See c, sec. 7.

From the *Journal of Discourses*, Vol. 17

What did God say in 1832? To what generation did
"God" refer? Was it the generation "then living"?
The early Mormons felt that they must return
quickly to Missouri and build the temple before
something happened, and they were confident that
they would return because of a revelation given in
1834. Did they return? Has the 1832 generation
passed away?

It is clear that Smith's temple prophecy was to
be fulfilled in the lifetime of those alive in 1832. The
1832 generation has passed away without building
the temple on the temple lot. Modern Mormons
object that Smith's prophecy did not refer to those
living in 1832, but to a future generation. This is a
weak attempt to avoid the fact that Smith prophesied falsely. All the historical documents relat-
ing to this prophecy clearly indicate that Smith and
his followers believed that the temple would be
built in their own lifetime. The temple lot is still an
empty field.

Most High God, we have not fulfilled his law; we have disobeyed the word which he gave through his servant Joseph, and hence the Lord has suffered us to be smitten and afflicted under the hands of our enemies.

Shall we ever return to the law of God? Yes. When? Why, when we will. We are agents; we can abide his law or reject it, just as long as we please, for God has not taken away your agency nor mine. But I will try to give you some information in regard to the time. God said, in the year 1832, before we were driven out of Jackson County, in a revelation which you will find here in this book, that before that generation should all pass away, a house of the Lord should be built in that county, (Jackson County), "upon the consecrated spot, as I have appointed; and the glory of God, even a cloud by day and a pillar of flaming fire by night shall rest upon the same." In another place, in the same revelation, speaking of the priesthood, he says that the sons of Moses and the sons of Aaron, those who had received the two priesthoods, should be filled with the glory of God upon Mount Zion, in the Lord's house, and should receive a renewing of their bodies, and the blessings of the Most High should be poured out upon them in great abundance.

This was given forty-two years ago. The generation then living was not only to commence a house of God in Jackson County, Missouri, but was actually to complete the same, and when it is completed the glory of God should rest upon it. Now, do you Latter-day Saints believe that? I do, and if you believe in these revelations you just as much expect the fulfillment of that revelation as of any one that God has ever given in these latter times, or in former ages. We look, just as much

for this to take place, according to the word of the Lord, as the Jews look to return to Palestine, and to re-build Jerusalem upon the place where it formerly stood. They expect to build a Temple there, and that the glory of God will enter into it; so likewise do we Latter-day Saints expect to return to Jackson County and to build a Temple there before the generation that was living forty-two years ago has all passed away. Well, then, the time must be pretty near when we shall begin that work. Now, can we be permitted to return and build up the waste places of Zion, establish the great central city of Zion in Jackson County, Mo., and build a Temple on which the glory of God will abide by day and by night, unless we return, not to the "new order," but to that law which was given in the beginning of this work? Let me answer the question by quoting one of these revelations again, a revelation given in 1834. The Lord, speaking of the return of his people, and referring to those who were driven from Jackson County, says—"They that remain shall return, they and their children with them to receive their inheritances in the land of Zion, with songs of everlasting joy upon their heads." There will be a few that the Lord will spare to go back there, because they were not all transgressors. There were only two that the Lord spared among Israel during their forty years travel—Caleb and Joshua. They were all that were spared, out of some twenty-five hundred thousand people, from twenty years old and upwards, to go into the land of promise. There may be three in our day, or a half dozen or a dozen spared that were once on that land who will be permitted to return with their children, grand-children and great-grand-children unto the waste places of Zion and build them

From the *Journal of Discourses*, Vol. 19

him this to satisfy his curiosity, for no man, we are told, had ever before witnessed such great things, and the Lord could not withhold them from him, because of his great faith. I do not believe, either, that this great man would have sought the Lord seeking to satisfy curiosity: but I told you, and I do believe, that He revealed to him many of his great and marvell...

doubt, were revealed to this man of God, and were commanded to be written, and will come forth when the generation has fully past away that were living in the year 1829—forty-eight years ago.

As regards the number of years by which a generation shall be measured, we have no special definite, period given...

> When will "all these things" come to pass? Did "this generation" refer to the people living in 1832 when the revelation was given? How many years have passed since the revelation? Since the people living in 1832 have died, what must we conclude about this prophecy's validity?

...of darkness that the world would be in before the Lord would set up this Church upon the earth again, and the persecutions that would come up on the former-day Saints, and how the Church would fall away and the Priesthood be taken away from among men; all these things were manifested to him, and he was commanded to write them. And if we had these things now which he wrote, I have not the least doubt we could read the future history of this Church, just the same as we can its past history; we could understand all the particulars until the wicked shall be destroyed from the earth, and we could see our future travels and our future tribulations and persecutions, and also our blessings that shall come upon us after the days of tribulations are ended; we could behold the glory of God that would rest upon Zion, and the resurrection of the righteous dead, and the coming of the Church of the First Born in the clouds of heaven, in connection with Jesus, and the coming of the ancient day Zion. All these things, I have no

son, etc., and when we come to average generations, according to the statistics of nations, we find them to be about thirty years to a generation; but when the Lord speaks in general terms, and says, This generation shall not pass away, until a House shall be built to his name, as is given in this "Book of Covenants," and a cloud should rest upon it; in that case I do not think he is limited to any definite period, but suffice it to say that the people living in 1832, when the revelation was given, will not all pass away; there will be some living when the House spoken of will be reared, on which the glory of God will rest. Already forty-five years have passed away since that revelation was given, concerning the building of that House. And when he says to Hyrum Smith, "Study my word, etc., until you have obtained all which I shall grant unto the children of men in this generation," I do not know how long that generation was intended, in the mind of God, to be, and I do not think there is any person in the Church that does know, unless the Lord has revealed

5. JOSEPH SMITH AND PROPHECY ON WORLD WAR AND THE DAY OF THE LORD

During the early 1830s, much public discussion over the slavery issue centered on the possibility that the Southern States would secede from the Union. It was feared that this would lead to civil war. In 1832, Joseph Smith echoed the public concern about a possible civil war. But he went further in his concern by actually prophesying that the war would take place and to what it would lead. Did he see this civil war as a world war or only as an American conflict? Did he prophesy that it would end with the coming of the day of the Lord? The documents can tell us what Smith said.

while the blade is yet tender (for verily your faith is weak), lest you destroy the wheat also.

7. Therefore, let the wheat and the tares grow to...

the har...

[overlaid note:] Soon after 1832, what would break out? Where would these wars break out? Upon how many nations would this war be poured out? What divine judgments would be poured out at this time? What would the consumption decreed do? What was coming? How soon was the day of the Lord to come? Did this prophecy come true?

9. For ye are lawful heirs, according to the flesh, and ... ave been hid fr... ith ...

... people Israel. The Lord ... hath said it. Amen.

SECTION 87.

REVELATION AND PROPHECY ON WAR, *given through Joseph Smith the Prophet, December 25, 1832.* —— *Wars predicted—Division between the Northern States and the Southern States—Great calamities in manifestation of the chastening hand of God.*

1. Verily, thus saith the Lord concerning the wars that will shortly come to pass, beginning at the rebellion of South Carolina, which will eventually terminate in the death and misery of many souls;

2. And the time will come that war will be poured out upon all nations, ᵃbeginning at this place.

3. For behold, the Southern States shall be divided against the Northern States, and the Southern States will call on other nations, even the nation of Great Britain, as it is called, and they shall also call upon other nations, in order to defend themselves against other nations; and then ᵇwar shall be poured out upon all nations.

4. And it shall come to pass, after many days, ᶜslaves shall rise up against their masters, who shall be marshaled and disciplined for war.

5. And it shall come to pass also that the ᵈremnants who are left of the land will marshal themselves, and shall become exceedingly angry, and shall vex the Gentiles with a sore vexation.

6. And thus, with the sword and by bloodshed the inhabitants of the earth shall mourn; and with famine, and plague, and earthquake, and the thunder of heaven, and the fierce and vivid lightning also, shall the inhabitants of the earth be made to feel the wrath, and indignation, and chastening hand of an Almighty

e, 107:41. 113:8. f, see k, sec. 38. Col. 3:3, 4. g, 27:6. 132:45. Mal.
4:6. Matt. 17:11. h, Obad. 21. Rom. 11:25—31. James 5:20.
SEC. 87: a, 130:12, 13. b, 45:69. c, 134:12. d, 109:65. 113:10. Al. 46:23.
3 Ne. 20:16. 21:12.

God, until the °consumption decreed hath made a full end of all nations;

7. That the cry of the saints, and of the 'blood of the saints, shall cease to come up into the ears of the Lord of Sabaoth, from the earth, to be avenged of their enemies.

8. Wherefore, stand ye in °holy places, and be not moved, until the *day of the Lord come; for behold, it cometh quickly, saith the Lord.   Amen.

SECTION 88.

REVELATION *given through Joseph Smith the Prophet, at Kirtland, Ohio, December 27, 1832. Designated by the Prophet, the Olive Leaf. See History of the Church, vol. 1, p. 302. —— Ministrations of the Comforter—The light of truth is the light of Christ—The spirit and the body constitute the soul—Parable of the man sending his servants into the field and visiting them in turn—Search for the truth through study and prayer enjoined—Testimony of the Elders to be followed by that of calamity—Scenes incident to the Lord's coming— The angels sounding their trumpets in turn as appointed—Duties of the Presidency of the School of the Prophets—The ordinance of washing of feet.*

1. Verily, thus saith the Lord unto you who have assembled yourselves together to receive his will concerning you:

2. Behold, this is pleasing unto your Lord, and the angels rejoice over you; the alms of your prayers have come up into the ears of the Lord of Sabaoth, and are recorded in the book of the names of the sanctified, even them of the celestial world.

3. Wherefore, I now send upon you another °Comforter, even upon you my friends, that it may abide in your hearts, even the Holy Spirit of promise; which other Comforter is the same that I promised unto my disciples, as is recorded in the testimony of John.

4. This Comforter is the promise which I give unto you of eternal life, even the glory of the celestial kingdom;

5. Which glory is that of the °church of the Firstborn, even of God, the holiest of all, through Jesus Christ his Son—

6. He that ascended up on high, as also he °descended below all things, in that he comprehended all things, that he might be in all and through all things, °the light of truth;

7. Which truth shineth. This is the light of Christ. As also he is °in the sun, and the light of the sun, and the power thereof by which it was made.

8. As also he is in the 'moon, and is the light of the moon, and the power thereof by which it was made;

9. As also the °light of the

e, see f and g, sec 1.   f, 58:53.   63:28—31.   1 Ne. 14:13.   22:14.   2 Ne. 27:2, 3.   28:10.   Morm. 8:27, 40, 41.   Eth. 8:22—24.   Rev. 6:9, 10.   18:24.   19:2. g, 45:32.   101:64.   h, see e, sec. 1, and b, sec. 2.   SEC. 88:   a, vers. 4, 5.   See h, sec. 42.   b, see a, sec. 1.   c, 122:8.   Eph. 4:9, 10.   d, vers. 7—13, 40, 41, 49, 50, 66, 67.   14:9.   84:44—48.   93:2, 8—17, 20, 23—39.   e, see d.   f, see d. g, see d.

6. JOSEPH SMITH AND SALEM, MASSACHUSETTS

By the mid-1830s, the Mormons had lost much of their personal property and wealth due to religious persecution and their resultant flights from one location to another. The debts of the Saints were mounting and a miracle was needed to pay all the outstanding bills. Smith claimed to have received a divine revelation from God that he was to go to Salem, Massachusetts. In this New England city he would find all the gold and silver they needed to pay their bills; he would also return with a great multitude of converts from that city. Did Smith find the predicted treasure of gold and silver in Salem? Did he return with the money to pay off the Saints' debts? Did he bring back with him a multitude of converts? What do the historic documents reveal?

3. His eyes were as a flame of fire; the hair of his head was white like the pure snow; his countenance shone above the brightness of the sun; and his voice was as the sound of the rushing of great waters, even the voice of Jehovah, saying:

4. I am the first and the last; I am he who liveth, I am he who was slain; I am your ~~~ with the F~~~

~~~ ~~~

~~~ ~~~ ~~~ the hearts of a~~~ ~~~y people rejoice, who have, with their might, built this house to my name.

7. For behold, I have accepted this house, and my name shall be here; and I will manifest myself to my people in mercy in this house.

8. Yea, I will *appear unto my servants, and speak unto them with mine own voice, if my people will keep my commandments, and do not pollute this holy house.

9. Yea, the hearts of thousands and tens of thousands shall greatly rejoice in consequence of the blessings which shall be poured out, and the *endowment with which my servants have been endowed in this house.

10. And the fame of this house shall spread to foreign lands; and this is the beginning of the bless-

ing which shall be poured out upon the heads of my people. Even so. Amen.

11. After this vision closed, the heavens were again opened unto us; and Moses appeared before us, and committed unto us the 'keys of the gathering of Israel from the f~~~ ~~~ the e~~~ ~~~ the ~~~ ~~~ he ~~~ ~~~ d, ~~~ ~~~ n ~~~ ~~~ say- ~~~ us and 'our seed all generations after us should be blessed.

13. After this vision had closed, another great and glorious vision burst upon us; for 'Elijah the prophet, who was taken to heaven without tasting death, stood before us, and said:

14. Behold, the time has fully come, which was spoken of by the mouth of Malachi—testifying that he [Elijah] should be sent, before the great and dreadful day of the Lord come—

15. To turn the hearts of the *fathers to the children, and the children to the fathers, lest the whole earth be smitten with a curse—

16. Therefore, the keys of this dispensation are committed into your hands; and by this ye may know that the great and dreadful day of the Lord is 'near, even at the doors.

What did Smith say he was going to get? What was to be given into Smith's hands? What would be his? Would the Saints pay off their debts?

SECTION 111.

REVELATION *given through Joseph Smith the Prophet, at Salem, Massachusetts, August 6, 1836. The Prophet with one of his Counselors and two other Elders had journeyed from Kirtland, Ohio, to Salem, Massachusetts; and, at their destination had entered upon the*

c, see e, sec. 45.   d, see o, sec. 50.   e, see x, sec. 38.   f, see k, sec. 6. 45:43.   133:13.   g, 133:26.   h, see g, sec. 27.   i, 124:57, 58.   j, see a, sec. 2.   k, see c, sec. 2.   l, see e, sec. 1.

work of teaching the people from house to house, and preaching publicly as opportunity presented. See History of the Church, vol. 2, p. 463. —— Directions for further labor—The Lord's assurances as to Zion.

1. I, the Lord your God, am not displeased with your coming this journey, notwithstanding your follies.

2. I have much treasure in this city for you, for the benefit of Zion, and many people in this city, whom I will gather out in due time for the benefit of Zion, through your instrumentality.

3. Therefore, it is expedient that you should form acquaintance with men in this city, as you shall be led, and as it shall be given you.

4. And it shall come to pass in due time that I will give this city into your hands, that you shall have power over it, insomuch that they shall not discover your secret parts; and its wealth pertaining to gold and silver shall be yours.

5. Concern   not   yourselves about your ªdebts, for I will give you power to pay them.

6. Concern   not   yourselves about Zion, for I will deal mercifully with her.

7. Tarry in this place, and in the regions round about;

8. And the place where it is my will that you should tarry, for the main, shall be signalized unto you by the peace and power of my Spirit, that shall flow unto you.

9. This place you may obtain by hire. And inquire diligently concerning the more ancient inhabitants and founders of this city;

10. For there are more treasures than one for you in this city.

11. Therefore, be ye as wise as serpents and yet without sin; and I will order all things for your good, as fast as ye are able to receive them. Amen.

SECTION 112.

REVELATION *given through Joseph Smith the Prophet, to Thomas B. Marsh, at Kirtland, Ohio, July 23, 1837. The word of the Lord unto Thomas B. Marsh, concerning the Twelve Apostles of the Lamb. The Prophet records that this revelation was received on the day on which the Gospel was first preached in England. Thomas B. Marsh was at this time president of the quorum of the Twelve Apostles. —— The Twelve to send the gospel abroad among all nations—They are to act under the direction of the First Presidency—Others may be authorized by the Twelve for ministry among the nations—The keys of power in the Priesthood committed to the First Presidency and the Twelve— The present designated as the dispensation of the fulness of times.*

1. Verily thus saith the Lord unto you my servant Thomas: I have heard thy prayers; and thine alms have come up as a memorial before me, in behalf of those, thy brethren, who were

a, 64:27—29.   See 2a, sec. 42.

2. I have much treasure in this city for you, for the benefit of Zion; and many people in this city whom I will gather out in due time for the benefit of Zion, through your instrumentality.

3. Therefore it is expedient that you should form acquaintance with men in this city, as you shall be led, and as it shall be given you:

4. And it shall come to pass in due time, that I will give this city into your hands; that you shall have power over it, insomuch that they shall not discover your secret parts; and its wealth pertaining to gold and silver shall be yours.

5. Concern not yourselves about your debts, for I will give you power to pay them.

6. Concern not yourselves about Zion, for I will deal mercifully with her.

7. Tarry in this place, and in the regions round about;

8. And the place where it is my will that you should tarry, for the main, shall be signalized unto you by the peace and power of my Spirit, that shall flow unto you.

9. This place you may obtain by hire, etc. And inquire diligently concerning the more ancient inhabitants and founders of this city;

10 For there are more treasures than one for you in this city;

11. Therefore be ye as wise as serpents and yet without sin, and I will order all things for your good, as fast as ye are able to receive them. Amen.

While here [at Salem] Brothers Brigham Young and Lyman E. Johnson arrived. Brother Young had been through New York, Vermont, and Massachusetts, in company with his brother Joseph Young. They visited their relations in this country, and baptized a good number into the Church; they remained in Boston two or three weeks, and baptized seventeen persons. We had a good visit with the brethren, for which I feel very thankful.

Thus I continued in Salem and vicinity until I returned to Kirtland, some time in the month of September. During this month the Church in Clay county, Missouri, commenced removing to their newly selected location on Shoal Creek, in the territory attached to Ray County.

During the quarter ending September 3rd, fifty-two Success of the Elders', six Priests', three Teachers', and Ministry. two Deacons' licenses were recorded in the license records, in Kirtland, Ohio, by Thomas Burdick. The intelligence from the Elders abroad was interesting.   Elder Parley P. Pratt still continued his labors in Upper Canada, Toronto, and vicinity, with good success. Elder Lyman E. Johnson had been laboring in New Brunswick, and other places on the sea-board; and on the 12th, 13th, and 14th of August a conference was held by Elders Brigham Young and Lyman E. John Newry, Maine, where seventeen numbering

> According to this account as told by Smith, did Smith act on his prophecy to go to Salem to obtain the money? Since Smith did not obtain the money or the converts in Salem as he predicted, he returned empty-handed. Some of his followers left him at this time because it was clear to them that Smith was a false prophet.

conferred blessings upon and preached the Gospel to many thousands.   They also visited their friends and relatives in the land of their nativity.   My cousin, George A. Smith, returned the same day from his mission to Richland County, Ohio.   Brother Heber C. Kimball returned to Kirtland, having been absent nearly five months, during which time he baptized thirty persons into the Church of the Latter-day Saints, this being in fulfillment of a blessing that I had conferred upon his head before he started on his mission.

Through the month of October the Saints continued to gather at Shoal Creek, Missouri, and my attention was particularly directed to the building up of Kirtland, and the spiritual interests of the Church.

Movements of the Saints in Missouri.

On the 2nd of November the brethren at Kirtland drew up certain articles of agreement, preparatory to the organization of a banking institution, to be called the "Kirtland Safety Society." *
President Oliver Cowdery was delegated to Philadelphia

Organization of Kirtland Safety Society

* "Kirtland Safety Society Bank" was the full title of the proposed institution, and Oliver Cowdery had the plates on which bank notes were to be printed so engraved.

7. JOSEPH SMITH AND ZION (INDEPENDENCE, MO.)

Joseph Smith prophesied that a Mormon city would be built in Missouri. The Mormons would build a large city which would be the headquarters of the church and the place of the central or great temple. He claimed to have received divine revelation that Zion would be built within that generation. Although they were violently driven out of the area, Smith prophesied that the Saints would return and build Zion. He even set dates for their return! Even after they settled in Salt Lake City, it was prophesied that they would return to Zion, Jackson County, Missouri. What exactly did Smith prophesy about Zion? Within what time limit would his predictions come true? Was there any other place where *the* temple could be built? Is the present city of Independence, Missouri, Zion? What about the boarding house where the physical descendants of Smith would live from generation to generation? Was it ever built? Is there a Mormon city, temple and boarding house in Jackson County, Missouri?

100

he shall be

In 1833, Smith prophesied that the Saints would return to what region? When was God's wrath to
be poured out? Upon whom? Would the Mormon
city, Zion, be built? Is there any other place which
God has appointed to be the headquarters of the
church? Did God's wrath pour out on all nations?
Did the people return and build Zion? Since God's
wrath was never "poured out" and the Saints never returned to build Zion as the headquarters of the
church, we must conclude that Joseph Smith
prophesied falsely.

SECTION 101.

REVELATION *given to Joseph Smith the Prophet, at Kirtland,
Ohio, December 16, 1833. At this time the Saints who had gathered
in Missouri were suffering great persecution. Mobs had driven them
from their homes in Jackson County, and some of the Saints had tried
to establish themselves in Van Buren County, but persecution followed
them. The main body of the Church was at that time in Clay County,
Missouri. Threats of death against individuals of the Church were
many. The people had lost household furniture, clothing, livestock
and other personal property, and many of their crops had been destroyed. See History of the Church, vol. 1, p. 456. —— Affliction permitted to befall the Saints because of their transgression—The Lord's
indignation to be poured out upon all nations—The pure in heart
among those who had been expelled from Zion to return—Other stakes
of Zion to be established—Blessed state incident to the millennial era
of peace—Parable of the nobleman and the olive-trees—Gathering of
the Saints to be continued—Those who have been oppressed by their
enemies to importune for redress—Creation of the Constitution of the
United States directed by the Lord—Parable of the woman and the
unjust judge.*

1. Verily I say unto you, concerning your brethren who have
been afflicted, and persecuted,
and °cast out from the land of
their inheritance—

2. I, the Lord, have suffered
the affliction to come upon them,
wherewith they have been afflicted, in consequence of ᵇtheir trans-
gressions;

3. Yet I will own them, and
they shall be mine in that day

c, 21:1. 124:94. d, 43:29. 84:99. 101:17, 18, 43, 74, 75. 103:1, 11, 13, 15.
105:1, 2, 9, 13, 16, 34. 109:51. 136:18. e, Rom. 8:28. Isa. 1:27. 35:10. 52:8.
59:20. Joel 2:23. Rev. 14:1. P. of G. P., Moses 7:62—64. SEC. 101: a, ver. 76.
64:30—36. 84:54—59. 103:2, 11. 104:51. 109:47. 121:23. b, vers. 3—9.

when I shall come to make up 'my jewels.

4. Therefore, they must needs be chastened and tried, even as Abraham, who was commanded to offer up his only son.

5. For all those who will not endure chastening, but deny me, cannot be sanctified.

6. Behold, I say unto you, there were jarrings, and contentions, and envyings, and strifes, and lustful and covetous desires among them; therefore by these things they ^dpolluted their inheritances.

7. They were slow to hearken unto the voice of the Lord their God; therefore, the Lord their God is ^eslow to hearken unto their prayers, to answer them in the day of their trouble.

8. In the day of their peace they esteemed lightly my counsel; but, in the ^fday of their trouble, of necessity they feel after me.

9. Verily I say unto you, notwithstanding their sins, my bowels are filled with compassion towards them. I will not utterly cast them off; and in the day of wrath I will ^gremember mercy.

10. I have sworn, and the decree hath gone forth by a former commandment which I have given unto you, that I would let ^hfall the sword of mine indignation in behalf of my people; and even as I have said, it shall come to pass.

11. Mine indignation is 'soon to be poured out without measure upon all nations; and this will I do when the cup of their iniquity is full.

12. And in that day all who are found upon the watch-tower,

or in other words, all mine Israel, shall be saved.

13. And they that have been scattered shall be ^jgathered.

14. And all they who have mourned shall be ^kcomforted.

15. And all they who have given their lives for my name shall be ^lcrowned.

16. Therefore, let your hearts be comforted concerning Zion; for all flesh is in mine hands; be still and know that I am God.

17. Zion shall not be ^mmoved out of her place, notwithstanding her children are scattered.

18. They that remain, and are pure in heart, shall return, and come to their inheritances, they and their children, with ⁿsongs of everlasting joy, to build up the waste places of Zion—

19. And all these things that the prophets might be fulfilled.

20. And, behold, there is none other place appointed than that which I have appointed; neither shall there be any other place appointed than that which I have appointed, for the work of the gathering of my saints—

21. Until the day cometh when there is found no more room for them; and then I have other places which I will appoint unto them, and they shall be called ^ostakes, for the curtains or the strength of Zion.

22. Behold, it is my will, that all they who call on my name, and worship me according to mine everlasting gospel, should ^pgather together, and stand in holy places;

23. And prepare for the revelation which is to come, when the veil of the covering of my temple, in my tabernacle, which hideth

c, see a, sec. 60.   d, 84:55—59.   e, vers. 39—42.   f, vers. 39—42, 44—54.
Hos. 5:15.   6:1—3.   g, vers. 10—19.   103:11—20.   h, see f and g, sec. 1.
i, see f and g, sec. 1.   j, see 2e, sec. 45.   k, 56:18—20.   Isa. 40: 1, 2.   l, Rev.
20:4.   m, vers. 20—22.   n, 45:71.   Isa. 35:10.   o, see e, sec. 82.   p, see j.
sec. 10.

Oliver Cowdery, Thomas Burdick and Orson Hyde, were nominated and appointed a committee by unanimous vote.

Brother Sylvester then said that he was willing to publish a confession in the *Star*.

OLIVER COWDERY, Clerk.

I wrote to Lyman Wight, Edward Partridge, John
The Prophet Reports His Vindication to the Elders in Missouri. Corrill, Isaac Morley, and others of the High Council of Zion, from Kirtland, August 16, 1834, as follows:

DEAR BRETH——

In 1834, Smith commanded his followers to be in readiness. Why? When would they move back to Jackson County, Missouri? Why did he prophesy that they would return in two years? They did not return to Zion by Sept. 11, 1836.

...... catalogue of charges
...... res himself; and the cry was Tyrant—Pope
—Usurper—Abuser of men—Angel—False Prophet—Prophesying lies in the name of the Lord—Taking consecrated monies—and every other lie to fill up and complete the catalogue. Such experiences may be necessary to perfect the Church, and render our traducers mete for the devourer, and the shaft of the destroying angel. In consequence of having to combat all these, I have not been able to regulate my mind, so as to give you counsel, and the information that you needed; but that God who rules on high, and thunders judgments upon Israel when they transgress, has given me power from the time I was born into the kingdom to stand; and I have succeeded in putting all gainsayers and enemies to flight, unto the present time; and notwithstanding the adversary laid a plan, which was more subtle than all others, as you will see by the next *Star*, I now swim in good, clean water, with my head out.

I shall now proceed to give you such counsel as the Spirit of the Lord may dictate. You will recollect that your business must be done by your High Council. You will recollect that the first Elders are to receive their endowment in Kirtland, before the redemption of Zion. You will recollect that   Council will have power to say who of the first Elders among the children of Zion are accounted worthy; and you will also recollect that you have my testimony in behalf of certain ones, previous to my departure. You will recollect that the sooner these ambassadors of the Most High are dispatched to bear testimony, to lift up a warning voice, and proclaim the everlasting Gospel, and to use every convincing proof and faculty with this generation, while on their journey to Kirtland—the better it will be for them and for Zion.   Inasmuch as the indignation of the people sleepeth for a while our time should be employed to the best advantage; although it is not the will of God, that these ambassadors should hold their peace after they have started upon their journey. They should arouse the sympathy of the people.

I would recommend to Brother Phelps, (if he be yet there,) to write a petition, such as will be approved by the High Council; and let every signer be obtained that can be, in the State of Missouri by them while they are on their journey to this place [Kirtland] that peradventure we may learn whether we have friends or not in these United States.

This petition is to be sent to the governor of Missouri, to solicit him to call on the President of the United States for a guard to protect our brethren in Jackson county, upon their own lands, from the insults and abuse of the mob.

And I would recommend to Brother Wight to enter complaint to the governor as often as he receives any insults or injury; and in case that they proceed to endeavor to take life, or tear down houses, and if the citizens of Clay county do not befriend us, to gather up the little army, and be set over immediately into Jackson county, and trust in God, and do the best he can in maintaining the ground.   But, in case the excitement continues to be allayed, and peace prevails, use every effort to prevail on the churches to gather to those regions and locate themselves, to be in readiness to move into Jackson county in two years from the eleventh of September next, which is the appointed time for the redemption of Zion.   If—verily I say unto you—if the Church with one united effort perform their duties; if they do this, the work shall be complete—if they do not this in all humility, making preparation from this time forth, like Joseph in Egypt, laying up store against the time of famine, every man having his tent, his horses, his chariots, his armory, his cattle, his family, and his whole substance in readiness against the time when it shall be said: To your tents, O Israel!   Let not this be noised abroad; let every heart beat in silence, and every mouth be shut.

Now, my beloved brethren, you will learn by this we have a great work to do, and but little time to do it in; and if we do not exert ourselves to the utmost in gathering up the strength of the Lord's house that this thing may be accomplished, behold there remaineth a scourge for the Church, even that they shall be driven from city to city, and the garden, it might be said, of the United States; and from Missouri to Illinois—all rich and productive States. What is the result of our removals? We came to a land that was a barren, uninviting desert, and what are the remar... come...

> What did the early Mormons believe about Zion? Did their predictions come true? The conclusion is forced upon us by the church's failure to return to Jackson County that they were following a false prophet.

...sign, that instead of this land being in many respects so superior, the fertility which formerly prevailed there would be restored. And when the day shall come, as come it will, when we shall go back—and we expect to go back to Jackson County, Missouri, and to lay the foundation of a temple, and to build a great city to be called the centre stake of Zion, as much as we expect to see the sun rise to-morrow; I say when that day shall come it will be found that that country will have its old fertility restored, and that and all the lands that the people of God will occupy will be healthy and fruitful; and the land of any people who will honor God by obeying this law of tithing will be made fruitful to them, God will bless their industry, and they will rejoice and prosper therein.

There are many things connected with this subject that might be touched upon. One thing I will mention before I sit down, and that is the growing tendency among this people to look after their own interests and to neglect the interests of the work of God. This remark has often been made to us: "When you Latter-day Saints increase in wealth, are surrounded by the fashions of the world, and the waves of civilization surge against your walls of barbarism, all your peculiarities will recede and melt away, and you will become like other people. Your plans... will disap...

...g to the re... of modern society. Now, there is a good deal of truth in this statement. If I thought we would become subject to the follies that now prevail I would have fears concerning the work of God and its perpetuity on the earth. If I thought that this people would lust after wealth, and that they would allow their feelings and their hearts to become set on the accumulation of money, and that they would think more of that than they do of God and his work, I would fear for its perpetuity. But God has said this work shall stand for ever, and that it shall not be given into the hands of another people, and on that account I do not entertain any fears as to the result. But there are individuals in this community who have given way to these feelings about tithing. When men are poor, it is noticed that they are punctual in paying it, but when they increase in wealth it is less so. For instance, when a man has ten thousand dollars it looks a big pile to give one thousand as tithing. If a man's tithing amounted to no more than five, ten, twenty, or even a hundred dollars, says he, "I can give that, but a thousand is a great amount," and when called upon to give a thousand, no, I will not say 'called upon," the difficulty is we are not called upon enough, there has been neglect in calling upon us; but when it comes

From the *Journal of Discourses*, Vol. 17

Who supposedly told Smith about a temple which would be built in Jackson County? In what generation would this temple be built? Was Smith referring to the generation then living? What did the early Mormons expect would happen? Was there a deadline which had to be met to avoid a false prophecy? Did they meet the deadline? Was this a *prophecy*? Will they build the city and temple in Jackson County? Must they do it to fulfill a prophetic revelation? The irrefutable facts that Zion and its temple were never built within "the generation then living" implicates Joseph Smith as a false prophet.

... will. We are agents; we can abide his law or reject it, just as long as we please, for God has not taken away your agency nor mine. But I will try to give you some information in regard to the time. God said, in the year 1832, before we were driven out of Jackson County, in a revelation which you will find here in this book, that before that generation should all pass away, a house of the Lord should be built in that county, (Jackson County,) "upon the consecrated spot, as I have appointed; and the glory of God, even a cloud by day and a pillar of flaming fire by night shall rest upon the same." In another place, in the same revelation, speaking of the priesthood, he says that the sons of Moses and the sons of Aaron, those who had received the two priesthoods, should be filled with the glory of God upon Mount Zion, in the Lord's house, and should receive a renewing of their bodies, and the blessings of the Most High should be poured out upon them in great abundance.

This was given forty-two years ago. The generation then living was not only to commence a house of God in Jackson County, Missouri, but was actually to complete the same, and when it is completed the glory of God should rest upon it.

Now, do you Latter-day Saints believe that? I do, and if you believe in these revelations you just as much expect the fulfillment of that revelation as of any one that God has ever given in these latter times, or in former ages. We look, just as much

... enter into it; so likewise do we Latter-day Saints expect to return to Jackson County and to build a Temple there before the generation that was living forty-two years ago has all passed away. Well, then, the time must be pretty near when we shall begin that work. Now, can we be permitted to return and build up the waste places of Zion, establish the great central city of Zion in Jackson County, Mo., and build a Temple on which the glory of God will abide by day and by night, unless we return, not to the "new order," but to that law which was given in the beginning of this work? Let me answer the question by quoting one of these revelations again, a revelation given in 1834. The Lord, speaking of the return of his people, and referring to those who were driven from Jackson County, says—"They that remain shall return, they and their children with them to receive their inheritances in the land of Zion, with songs of everlasting joy upon their heads." There will be a few that the Lord will spare to go back there, because they were not all transgressors. There were only two that the Lord spared among Israel during their forty years travel—Caleb and Joshua. They were all that were spared, out of some twenty-five hundred thousand people, from twenty years old and upwards, to go into the land of promise. There may be three in our day, or a half dozen or a dozen spared that were once on that land who will be permitted to return with their children, grand-children and great-grand-children unto the waste places of Zion and build them

handcuffs, and chains, and shack-
les, and fetters of hell.

9. Therefore it is an imperative duty that we owe, not only
to our own wives and children,
but to the widows and fatherless,
whose husbands and fathers have
been murdered under its iron
hand;

10. Which dark and ___
ing deeds are ___
hell ___

___
___
ti___
ri___
pu___

the___
ties ___
blin ___ by the subtle craftiness
of men, whereby they lie in wait
to deceive, and who are only kept
from the truth because they know
not where to find it—

13. Therefore, that we should
waste and wear out our lives in
bringing to light all the hidden
things of darkness, wherein we
know them; and they are truly
manifest from heaven—

14. These sh___ ___ at-
tended ___ ___ ss.

___ as
___ ch
___ s-
___ s

___ ___me
___ being kept
___ the wind and the
___aves.

17. Therefore, dearly beloved
brethren, let us cheerfully do all
things that lie in our power; and
then may we stand still, with the
utmost assurance, to see the salvation of God, and for his arm to
be revealed.

> The Mormons fled from Missouri to Illinois. What
> was to be built for strangers in Nauvoo, Illinois?
> What else was to be built there? Was Nauvoo ever
> completed? Nauvoo's boarding house and temple
> were never built, in contradiction of Joseph
> Smith's prophecy.

SECTION 124.

REVELATION *given to Joseph Smith the Prophet, at Nauvoo, Illinois,
January 19, 1841. Because of increasing persecutions and illegal pro-
cedures against them by public officers, the Saints had been compelled
to leave Missouri. The exterminating order issued by Lilburn W.
Boggs, Governor of Missouri, dated October 27, 1838, had left them
no alternative. See History of the Church, vol. 3, p. 175. In 1841,
when this revelation was given, the city of Nauvoo, occupying the site
of the former village of Commerce, Illinois, had been built up by the
Saints, and here the headquarters of the Church had been established. —— Proclamation to the president of the United States, the
governors of the States, and to the rulers of all nations—Blessed state
of former members of the Church who had died—George Miller called
to the bishopric—A house of entertainment for strangers to be erected—
A Temple to be built at Nauvoo—No baptismal font upon the earth
for the administration of baptisms for the dead—Reason for the command to Moses to build a tabernacle in the wilderness—Promise of
revelations concerning sacred things thus far hidden—Men who prevent*

pleased with him, and that he should be with you;

13. Let him, therefore, hearken to your counsel, and I will bless him with a multiplicity of blessings; let him be faithful and true in all things from henceforth, and he shall be great in mine eyes;

14. But let him remember that his ᵍstewardship will I require at his hands.

15. And again, verily I say unto you, blessed is my servant Hyrum Smith; for I, the Lord, love him because of the integrity of his heart, and because he loveth that which is right before me, saith the Lord.

16. Again, let my servant John C. Bennett help you in your labor in sending my word to the kings and people of the earth, and stand by you, even you my servant Joseph Smith, in the hour of affliction; and his reward shall not fail if he receive counsel.

17. And for his love he shall be great, for he shall be mine if he do this, saith the Lord. I have seen the work which he hath done, which I accept if he continue, and will crown him with blessings and great glory.

18. And again, I say unto you that it is my will that my servant Lyman Wight should continue in preaching for Zion, in the spirit of meekness, confessing me before the world; and I will bear him up as on eagles' wings; and he shall beget glory and honor to himself and unto my name.

19. That when he shall finish his work I may receive him unto myself, even as I did my servant David Patten, who is with me at this time, and also my servant Edward Partridge, and also my aged servant Joseph Smith, Sen., who sitteth with Abraham at his right hand, and blessed and holy is he, for he is mine.

20. And again, verily I say unto you, my servant George Miller is without guile; he may be trusted because of the integrity of his heart; and for the love which he has to my testimony I, the Lord, love him.

21. I therefore say unto you, I seal upon his head the office of a bishopric, like unto my servant Edward Partridge, that he may receive the consecrations of mine house, that he may administer blessings upon the heads of the poor of my people, saith the Lord. Let no man despise my servant George, for he shall honor me.

22. Let my servant George, and my servant Lyman, and my servant John Snider, and others, build a ʰhouse unto my name, such a one as my servant Joseph shall show unto them, upon the place which he shall show unto them also.

23. And it shall be for a house for boarding, a house that strangers may come from afar to lodge therein; therefore let it be a good house, worthy of all acceptation, that the weary traveler may find health and safety while he shall contemplate the word of the Lord; and the corner-stone I have appointed for Zion.

24. This house shall be a healthful habitation if it be built unto my name, and if the governor which shall be appointed unto it shall not suffer any pollution to come upon it. It shall be holy, or the Lord your God will not dwell therein.

25. And again, verily I say unto you, let 'all my saints come from afar.

26. And send ye swift messengers, yea, chosen messengers, and say unto them: Come ye, with all your gold, and your silver, and your precious stones, and with all your antiquities; and with all who have knowledge of antiquities, that will come, may come, and bring the box-tree, and the fir-tree, and the pine-tree, together with all the precious trees of the earth;

27. And with iron, with copper, and with brass, and with zinc, and with all your precious things of the earth; and build a house to my name, for the ʲMost High to dwell therein.

28. For there is not a place found on earth that he may come to and restore again that which was lost unto you, or which he hath taken away, even the fulness of the priesthood.

29. For a ᵏbaptismal font there is not upon the earth, that they, my saints, may be ˡbaptized for those who are dead—

30. For this ordinance belongeth to my house, and cannot be acceptable to me, only in the days of your poverty, wherein ye are not able to build a house unto me.

31. But I command you, all ye my saints, to build a house unto me; and I grant unto you a sufficient time to build a house unto me; and during this time your ᵐbaptisms shall be acceptable unto me.

32. But behold, at the end of this appointment your ⁿbaptisms for your dead shall not be acceptable unto me; and if you do not these things at the end of the appointment ye shall be ᵒrejected as a church, with your dead, saith the Lord your God.

33. For verily I say unto you, that after you have had sufficient time to build a house to me, wherein the ordinance of ᵖbaptizing for the dead belongeth, and for which the same was instituted from before the foundation of the world, ᵍyour baptisms for your dead cannot be acceptable unto me;

34. For therein are the keys of the holy priesthood ordained, that you may receive honor and glory.

35. And ʳafter this time, your baptisms for the dead, by those who are scattered abroad, are not acceptable unto me, saith the Lord.

36. For it is ordained that in Zion, and in her stakes, and in Jerusalem, those places which I have appointed for refuge, shall be the ˢplaces for your baptisms for your dead.

37. And again, verily I say unto you, how shall your ᵗwashings be acceptable unto me, except ye perform them in a house which you have built to my name?

38. For, for this cause I ᵘcommanded Moses that he should build a tabernacle, that they should bear it with them in the wilderness, and to build a house in the land of promise, that those ordinances might be revealed which had been hid from before the world was.

39. Therefore, verily I say unto you, that your ᵛanointings, and your washings, and your baptisms for the dead, and your solemn assemblies, and your memorials for your sacrifices by the sons of Levi, and for your oracles in your

j, 97:15—17.   k, vers. 30—36, 39.   Secs. 127, 128.   1 Cor. 15:29.   l, see k.
m, see k.   n, ver. 29.   o, ver. 33.   p, see k.   q, see k.   r, ver. 32.   s, ver. 30.   t, ver. 39.   88:138—141.   u, Ex. 25:1—9.   1 Chron. chaps. 28, 29. v, 88:74, 139—141.

109

cration, so long as they repent not, and hate me, saith the Lord your God.

53. And this I make an example unto you, for your consolation concerning all those who have been commanded to do a work and have been ᵇʰindered by the hands of their enemies, and by oppression, saith the Lord your God.

54. For I am the Lord your God, and will save all those of your brethren who have been pure in heart, and have been slain in the land of Missouri, saith the Lord.

55. And again, verily I say unto you, I command you again to build a house to my name, even in this place, that you may ᶜprove yourselves unto me that ye are faithful in all things whatsoever I command you, that I may bless you, and crown you with honor, immortality, and eternal life.

56. And now I say unto you, as pertaining to my boarding house which I have commanded you to build for the boarding of strangers, let it be built unto my name, and let my name be named upon it, and let my servant Joseph and his house have place therein, from generation to generation.

57. For

generation to generation, forever and ever, saith the Lord.

60. And let the name of that house be called Nauvoo House; and let it be a delightful habitation for man, and a resting-place for the ʰweary traveler, that he may contemplate the glory of Zion, and the glory of this, the corner-stone thereof;

61. That he may receive also the counsel from those whom I have set to be as plants of renown, and as watchmen upon her walls.

62. Behold, verily I say unto you, let my servant George Miller, and my servant Lyman Wight, and my servant John Snider, and my servant Peter Haws, organize themselves, and appoint one of them to be a president over their quorum for the purpose of building that house.

63. And they shall form a constitution, whereby they may receive stock for the building of that house.

64. And they shall not receive less than fifty dollars for a share of stock in that house, and they shall be permitted to receive fifteen thousand dollars from any one man for

Is there any other place on earth where the temple can be built where God will restore the fullness of the priesthood? Once the time limit is past, what will God do to the Mormon Church if it has not built the temple at Nauvoo? Can baptisms be valid elsewhere if the temple is not built? Whose descendants shall live in Nauvoo House from generation to generation? Since the temple and boarding house were never built, what implication can be drawn regarding Joseph Smith's prophecies?

ze, ver. 57.   110:12.

110

From the *Journal of Discourses*, Vol. 17

Even after the Mormons were settled in Salt Lake City, Utah, did they prophesy that they would return to Jackson County? The prophesied return to Zion was restricted to "the generation then living in 1832" (vol. 17, p. 111), but that generation has passed away without seeing the fulfillment of Smith's prophecy.

... going from one part of this nation to another, peaceably and quietly, purchasing the land and locating upon it? I think not. "But," says one, "perhaps they will not allow you to purchase the land." The Lord will take care of that; that is in the hands of the Lord. That same being who will assist in the building of a great city on the western boundaries of the State of Missouri, has all power; and when we purchase the land, and go and take possession of it, I do not think we will be driven from our own lands, if we mind our own business and do not meddle with our neighbors' business, and do not undertake to injure them in their rights and privileges, guaranteed to them by the Constitution of our country. If we conduct ourselves in a peaceable manner, I do not see why we may not dwell there as well as other citizens. We have the strongest assurance that such will be the case. These were promises made to us, before there were a hundred persons in this Church. It was promised that we should have a land as an inheritance; but we were commanded of God, to purchase the land. Now, when the time comes for purchasing this land, we will have means. How this means will be brought about is

... Latter-day Saints till they will scarcely know what to do with it. I will here again prophesy on the strength of former revelation that there are no people on the face of the whole globe, not even excepting London, Paris, New York, or any of the great mercantile cities of the globe—there are no people now upon the face of the earth, so rich as the Latter-day Saints will be in a few years to come. Having their millions; therefore they will purchase the land, build up cities, towns and villages, build a great capital city, at headquarters, in Jackson County, Missouri. Will we have a temple there? Yes; will we have a beautiful city? Yes, one of the most beautiful cities that will ever be erected on the continent of America will be built up by the Latter-day Saints in Jackson County, Missouri. Consequently, when congressmen and statesmen, and the great men of our nation, want to know what the future destiny of the Latter-day Saints will be, let them remember the words of your humble servant, who has addressed you this afternoon; for they will come to pass—they will be fulfilled. We have seen too many revelations fulfilled, already, to be mistaken in regard to these matters. Amen.

From the *Journal of Discourses*, Vol. 18

around in ancient times, and taught the people from house to house and synagogue to synagogue. And in that day there shall be one Lord, and his name one. There will not be any heathen gods, for there will be no heathens; no idolatrous worship, but one Lord, and his name one.

And this water which breaks ~~~ from th~ "~~~~~~~~~~~~~~

~~~ sea; in other words half towards the Dead Sea and half toward the Mediterranean.

From that day forward there shall be written upon the bells of the horses and upon the vessels of the house of the Lord,—"Holiness to the Lord;" and thenceforth all the people who are spared from the nations round about, will have to go up to Jerusalem year by year to worship the King, the Lord of Hosts.

These are some of the grand events spoken of in this Bible; these are events that the Latter-day Saints believe in, and that so far as it lies in their power, they are trying to fulfill. If we are not Jews we are not required to go to old Jerusalem, but we are required to build up a Zion; that is spoken of as well as the building of Jerusalem. Zion is to be built up in the mountains in the last days, not at Jerusalem. Read the fortieth chapter of Isaiah, where he speaks of the glory of the Lord being revealed, and all flesh to see him when he comes the second time, and how the mountains and hills should be lowered and the valleys be exalted; and in the same chapter, the Prophet also says that, before

that great and terrible day of the Lord Zion is required to get up into the high mountains. Isaiah predicts this. Says he, in his fortieth chapter—"Oh Zion, thou that bringest good tidings, get thee up into the high mountains."

Thus you see th~~ ~

Where will the headquarters of the Mormon Church be? Have the Saints returned and built the city and temple of Zion? The church's headquarters is in Salt Lake City, not Jackson County, Missouri.

~~~~ of the ocean, scattered over four hundred miles of Territory, north and south, and you are extending your settlements continually, and are building up some two hundred towns, cities and villages in the mountains of the great American desert, fulfilling the prophecies of the holy Prophets.

By and by you will leave this country. Says one—"What, are the Mormons going to leave Utah?" Oh yes, most of us; we are going to leave, but we shall disappoint some of you. You want to know which way we are going? We are going by and by eastward. I do not say that we shall go directly from this city eastward, but we shall, after a while, be in Jackson County, in the western borders of Missouri. Why are we going there? Because it is the great central gathering place for the Saints of latter days, for all that will be gathered from South America, Central America, Mexico, the Canadas, and from all the nations of the Gentiles—their head quarters will be in Jackson County, in the State of Missouri. We shall roll down from the mountains, and though we may be considered but a little stone cut out of the mountains without human ingenuity, without mankind under-

8. JOSEPH SMITH'S PROPHECY REGARDING DAVID PATTEN

In the spring of 1838, Smith prophesied that David Patten would go out on a missionary tour with him and several others in the spring of 1839. Patten was told to prepare for the trip because he would accompany Smith and a select group of men. The only problem with this prophecy is that Patten was killed that winter and never made it alive to the spring. He did not accompany Smith on his missionary tour. What did the prophecy say? Who was Patten to accompany? Since he did not go on the predicted tour, what does this tell us about Smith's prophecy? Is this prophecy a false prophecy?

SECTION 113.

ANSWERS *to certain questions on Scripture, given by Joseph Smith the Prophet, March, 1838.*

1. Who is the Stem of Jesse spoken of in the 1st, 2d, 3d, 4th, and 5th verses of the 11th chapter of Isaiah?

2. Verily thus saith the Lord: It is Christ.

3. What is the rod spoke~~n~~ in the first v~~erse~~

~~ch~~

1 ~~
C
o
o1
w~~

~~5. What~~ is the root of Jesse spoken of in the 10th verse of the 11th chapter?

6. Behold, thus saith the Lord, it is a descendant of Jesse, as well as of Joseph, unto whom rightly belongs the priesthood, and the keys of the kingdom, for an ᵃensign, and for the gathering of my people in the last days.

7. Questions by Elias Higbee: What is meant by the command in Isaiah, 52d chapter, 1st verse,

which saith: Put on thy strength, O Zion—and what people had Isaiah reference to?

8. He had reference to th~~ose~~ whom God shoul~~d~~ ~~...~~ ast days ~~wh...~~ ~~...er,~~ ~~n,~~ ~~1;~~ ~~o~~ ~~t~~ ~~to~~ ~~...~~ sne had lost.

~~...~~ ~~..~~at are we to understand by Zion loosing herself from the bands of her neck; 2d verse?

10. We are to understand that the scattered ᵇremnants are exhorted to return to the Lord from whence they have fallen; which if they do, the promise of the Lord is that he will speak to them, or give them revelation. See the 6th, 7th, and 8th verses. The bands of her neck are the curses of God upon her, or the remnants of Israel in their scattered condition among the Gentiles.

SECTION 114.

REVELATION *given through Joseph Smith the Prophet, at Far West, Missouri, April 17, 1838. —— Directions to David W. Patten—Positions occupied by the unfaithful to be given to others.*

1. Verily thus saith the Lord: It is wisdom in my servant David W. Patten, that he settle up all his business as soon as he possibly can, and make a disposition of his merchandise, that he may perform a mission unto me next spring, in company with others, even twelve including himself, to testify of my name and bear glad tidings unto all the world.

2. For verily thus saith the Lord, that inasmuch as there are those among you who ᵃdeny my name, others shall be planted in their stead and receive their bishopric. Amen.

a, see i, sec. 45.   b, see d, sec. 87.   SEC. 114: a, 118:1, 6.

114

a company to disperse the mob and retake their prisoners, whom, it was reported, they intended to murder that Crooked River Battle. night. The trumpet sounded, and the brethren were assembled on the public square about midnight, when the facts were stated, and about seventy-five volunteered to obey the judge's order, under command of Captain David W. Patten, who immediately commenced their march on horseback, hoping without the loss of blood to surprise and scatter the camp, retake the prisoners and prevent the ....

Smith prophesied about Patten in April of 1838. He was to go out with him and eleven others in the spring of 1839. When did Patten die? Since he died in October of 1838, he could not have gone out on tour with Smith and eleven others in the spring of 1839. The modern Mormon response to this obvious false prophecy by Joseph Smith is to claim that Patten fulfilled Smith's prophecy by being a missionary in the *spirit* world! The fact that Smith prophesied that Patten would leave on a missionary tour *with* Smith and other human companions rules out this attempt to avoid the irrefutable fact that Smith's prophecy was false.

.... under the bank of the river, below their tents. It was yet so dark that little could be seen by looking at the west, while the mob looking towards the dawning light, could see Patten and his men, when they fired a broadside, and three or four of the brethren fell. Captain Patten ordered the fire returned, which was instantly obeyed, to great disadvantage in the darkness which yet continued. The fire was repeated by the mob, and returned by Captain Patten's company, who gave the watchword "God and Liberty." Captain Patten then ordered a charge, which was instantly obeyed. The parties immediately came in contact, with their swords, and the mob were soon put to flight, crossing the river at the ford and such places as they could get a chance. In the pursuit, one of the mob fled from behind a tree, wheeled, and shot Captain Patten, who instantly fell, mortally wounded, having received a large ball in his bowels.

The ground was soon cleared, and the brethren gathered up a wagon or two, and making beds therein of tents, etc, took their wounded and retreated towards Far West.   Three brethren were wounded in the bowels, one in the neck, one in the shoulder, one through the hips, one through both thighs, one in the arms, all by musket shot. One had his arm broken by a sword.   Brother Gideon Carter was shot in the head, and left dead on the ground so defaced that the brethren did not know him.   Bogart reported that he had lost one man.   The three prisoners were released and returned with the brethren to Far West. Captain Patten was carried some of the way in a litter, but it caused so much distress that he begged to be left by the way side.   He was carried into Brother Winchester's, three miles from the city of Far West, where he died that night.   Patrick O'Banion died soon after, and Brother Carter's body was also brought from Crooked river, when it was discovered who he was.

List of Casualties. Death of Patten and O'Banion.

I went with my brother Hyrum and Lyman Wight to meet the brethren on their return, near Log creek, where I saw Captain Patten in a most distressing condition. His wound was incurable.

Brother David Patten was a very worthy man, beloved by all good men who knew him.   He was one of the Twelve Apostles, and died as he had lived, a man of God, and strong in the faith of a glorious resurrection, in a world where mobs will have no power or place.   One of his last expressions to his wife was—"Whatever you do else, O! do not deny the faith."

The Prophet's Reflections on the Death of David W. Patten.

How different his fate to that of the apostate, Thomas

Conclusion

We have examined the historical and factual evidence which documents eight false prophecies of Joseph Smith. According to Deut. 18:20-22, just one false prophecy is sufficient to identify a false prophet. While there are over sixty false prophecies of Joseph Smith which have been documented, these eight prophecies are sufficient to demonstrate beyond all reasonable doubt that Joseph Smith was *not* a prophet of God.

The implications of our conclusion concerning Joseph Smith's claim to be God's latter-day prophet are far-reaching and deeply radical, especially for Mormons.

If Smith is a fraud, and the historical documents confirm this to be the fact, then the entire Mormon religion collapses like a house of cards. There is no middle ground. It is either one way or the other.

What then can a sincere Mormon do once he or she discovers that Joseph Smith was a false prophet?

The answer does not lie in attaching oneself to another organization or church. The answer lies in the person and work of Jesus Christ. He is the incarnate Son of God, conceived by the Holy Spirit in the womb of the Virgin Mary. He is God the Son, second person of the Holy Trinity.

Once a person sees that Joseph Smith was a false prophet, he must renounce all Mormon doctrines, baptisms, priesthoods and relationships. *The Book of Mormon, The Pearl of Great Price* and *Doctrine and Covenants* must be viewed as spurious. He must turn to the Scriptures alone as the final authority in all matters of faith, life and practice.

The crucial issue which confronts every Mormon is, "What shall I do with Jesus?" Once all reliance on Joseph Smith is abandoned, total reliance on Christ alone through faith can begin.

WHAT SHOULD EVERY MORMON KNOW?

1. *That he is a sinner under the wrath of God.*

> For all have sinned, and come short of the glory of God. (Rom. 3:23)

> For the wages of sin is death; but the gift of God is eternal life through Jesus Christ our Lord. (Rom. 6:23)

2. *That God manifested His love for us by sending His only Son to be our Savior.*

> For God so loved the world, that he gave his only begotten Son, that whosoever believeth in him should not perish, but have everlasting life. (John 3:16)

> He that believeth on him is not condemned: but he that believeth not is condemned already, because he hath not believed in the name of the only begotten Son of God. (John 3:18)

> For when we were yet without strength, in due time Christ died for the ungodly. For scarcely for a righteous man will one die: yet peradventure for a good man some would even dare to die. But God commendeth his love toward us, in that, while we were yet sinners, Christ died for us. (Rom. 5:6-8)

> In this was manifested the love of God toward us, because that God sent his only begotten Son into the world, that we might live through him. (1 John 4:9)

3. *That we cannot be saved by our works such as baptism.*

> As it is written, There is none righteous, no, not one: there is none that understandeth, there is none that seeketh after God. They are all gone out of the way, they are together become unprofitable; there is none that doeth good, no, not one. (Rom. 3:10-12)

Therefore by the deeds of the law there shall no flesh be justified in his sight: for by the law is the knowledge of sin. But now the righteousness of God without the law is manifested, being witnessed by the law and the prophets; even the righteousness of God which is by faith of Jesus Christ unto all and upon all them that believe: for there is no difference. (Rom. 3:20-22)

What shall we say then that Abraham our father, as pertaining to the flesh, hath found? For if Abraham were justified by works, he hath whereof to glory; but not before God. For what saith the scripture? Abraham believed God, and it was counted unto him for righteousness. Now to him that worketh is the reward not reckoned of grace, but of debt. But to him that worketh not, but believeth on him that justifieth the ungodly, his faith is counted for righteousness. (Rom. 4:1-5)

Therefore being justified by faith, we have peace with God through our Lord Jesus Christ. (Rom. 5:1)

For by grace are ye saved through faith; and that not of yourselves: it is the gift of God: not of works, lest any man should boast. (Eph. 2:8, 9)

Not by works of righteousness which we have done, but according to his mercy he saved us, by the washing of regeneration, and renewing of the Holy Ghost. (Titus 3:5)

4. *We are saved by receiving Jesus Christ as our personal Lord and Savior.*

But as many as received him, to them gave he power to become the sons of God, even to them that believe on his name. (John 1:12)

That if thou shalt confess with thy mouth the Lord Jesus, and shalt believe in thine heart that God hath raised him from the dead, thou shalt be saved. For with the heart man believeth unto righteousness;

and with the mouth confession is made unto salvation. (Rom. 10:9, 10)

5. *There is a heaven to gain and a hell to shun.*

When the Son of man shall come in his glory, and all the holy angels with him, then shall he sit upon the throne of his glory: and before him shall be gathered all nations: and he shall separate them one from another, as a shepherd divideth his sheep from the goats: and he shall set the sheep on his right hand, but the goats on the left. Then shall the King say unto them on his right hand, Come, ye blessed of my Father, inherit the kingdom prepared for you from the foundation of the world. (Matt. 25:31-34)

Then shall he also say unto them on the left hand, Depart from me, ye cursed, into everlasting fire, prepared for the devil and his angels. (Matt. 25:41)

And these shall go away into everlasting punishment: but the righteous into life eternal. (Matt. 25:46)

6. *There is no other name under heaven whereby we must be saved than the name Jesus Christ. The name "Joseph Smith" cannot save anyone.*

. . . Sirs, what must I do to be saved? And they said, Believe on the Lord Jesus Christ, and thou shalt be saved, and thy house. (Acts 16:30-31)

Neither is there salvation in any other: for there is none other name under heaven given among men, whereby we must be saved. (Acts 4:12)

For there is one God, and one mediator between God and men, the man Christ Jesus. (1 Tim. 2:5)

Let the reader seriously consider these six facts, for upon them rests salvation in this life and in the life to come.

Sola Deo Gloria—to God alone be glory.

NOTES

NOTES

NOTES

NOTES

OTHER BOOKS AVAILABLE ON CULTS AND THE OCCULT

Order from your local bookstore or Bethany House Publishers.